15
TWO-BLOCK
Quilts

*Unlock the Secrets
of Secondary Patterns*

CLAUDIA OLSON

C&T PUBLISHING

© 2002 Claudia Olson
Editor-in-Chief: Darra Williamson
Developmental Editor: Pamela Mostek
Technical Editor: Karyn Hoyt-Culp, Joyce Engels Lytle
Copyeditor/Proofreader: Laura Reinstatler/Susan Nelsen
Cover Designer: Christina Jarumay
Book Designer: Rohani Design
Design Director: Diane Pedersen
Illustrator: Richard Sheppard
Front Cover Image: *Eight-Point Puzzle*
Back Cover Images: *Chrun Dash Memories, Pine Burr Star, and Fancy Corn and Beans*
Production Assistant: Kristy A. Konitzer
Photography: Jason Getzin
Published by C&T Publishing, Inc., P.O. Box 1456, Lafayette, California 94549

Attention Teachers: C&T Publishing, Inc. encourages you to use this book as a text for teaching. Contact us at 800-284-1114 or www.ctpub.com for more information about the C&T Teachers Program.

We take great care to ensure that the information included in this book is accurate and presented in good faith, but no warranty is provided nor results guaranteed. Since we have no control over the choices of materials or procedures used, neither the author nor C&T Publishing, Inc. shall have any liability to any person or entity with respect to any loss or damage caused directly or indirectly by the information contained in this book. For your convenience, we post an up-to-date listing of corrections on our web page (www.ctpub.com). If a correction is not already noted, please contact our customer service department at ctinfo@ctpub.com or at PO Box 1456, Lafayette, CA 94549.

Trademarked™ and Registered Trademark® names are used throughout this book. Rather than use the symbols with every occurrence of a trademark and registered trademark name, we are using the names only in the editorial fashion and to the
benefit of the owner, with no intention of infringement.

Library of Congress Cataloging-in-Publication Data

Olson, Claudia
    15 two-block quilts : unlock the secrets of secondary
patterns / Claudia Olson.
        p. cm.
    Includes index.
    ISBN 1-57120-147-5 (paper trade)
    1. Patchwork—Patterns. 2. Patchwork quilts—Design.
I. Title: Fifteen two-block quilts. I. Title.
TT835 .O5 2002
746.46'041—dc21

                                    2002005726

Printed in Singapore
10 9 8 7 6 5 4 3 2

I would like to dedicate 15 Two-Block Quilts to those who encouraged me and believed in my ability to do this work. They are Jill Therriault, Trudee Barritt, and Pat Peyton.

Acknowledgments

This book was truly a group effort. Without the kind help and encouragement of my good quilting friends who volunteered to make quilts, it would not have been possible.

I would like to express my deepest appreciation to the following quilters: Martha Robertson, Judy Lundberg, LaVanche Rhodes, Sandy Ashbrook, Doni Palmgren, Katherine Storrs, Terry Vaughan, Jane Wheeler, Lesley Allan, Mary Rosendaal, Beth Miracle, Debbie Koehnen, Brooke Thompsen, Mary Thompsen, Trudee Barritt, Alice Reathaford, Pam James, Linda Riesterer, Louise Brown, Karen Sinn, Barbara Vincent, Margaret Jack, Carolyn Kirkpatrick, Pat Peyton, and Marie Tiedemann.

A special thank you to Jill Therriault and Lynn Pittsinger for their incredible machine quilting skills and for helping me meet my deadlines.

Thanks to my family for their help and understanding. In particular, I would like to express my appreciation to my sister, Pat Peyton, who helped me walk through some tricky ideas and volunteered to make several projects for the book. Thanks also to the extra help that my husband, Greg, and children, Andrea and Kelson, gave me during particularly busy writing times.

More thanks go to Donna Carroll and Brenda Geren who cheerfully helped me copy multiple pages of my instructions.

A very special thank you goes to Jason Getzin, my photographer, for all the time and talent that he invested in this project to make the photos turn out so wonderfully.

Finally, I would like to thank those who helped with the various book and pattern making tasks. My sincere gratitude is sent to the staff and editors of C&T Publishing for believing in me and for coaching me through the various bookmaking steps.

Contents

Introduction

You've seen them in magazines and at quilt shows. You've probably even stood in front of these eye-catching two-block quilts and marveled at the complexities. Maybe you've even wondered why certain quilts were a success or why the quilters chose to combine those particular two blocks.

I have done the same thing. I realized, in fact, that I was doing a tremendous amount of staring at such quilts, marking them in my magazines and photographing them at quilt shows. I would look up the blocks in my quilt block dictionaries and dream about the possibilities of other, similar blocks.

Then, I decided to put my thoughts into action. I drew the blocks side by side to see what would happen. Then I tried them on my computer. When they interacted nicely or made a secondary pattern, I rejoiced! I made a couple of the quilts, sometimes with success and other times with disappointing results. I began to ask more questions. Why was one quilt design a success and the other a flop? Why did one design look wonderful on paper and then not work in the fabrics I had chosen?

I learned that while some blocks might be the same size, they may not complement each other. Some blocks may compete with each other in design or color. Spatial relationships, which are important for balance, either were pleasing or confusing. Also, certain colors that look good in drawings or on the computer look terrible in fabric!

By experimenting and studying I did come up with some great ideas for answering these questions, and I am excited to share them with you in 15 *Two-Block Quilts*. When you are through reading "Two-Block Formulas," you may want to tackle a design of your own. Sewing together your own design is challenging and fulfilling. Or you may prefer to make one of the two-block quilts I've designed for this book. Either way, I know you're going to love the quilt you create, and you're sure to grow in your knowledge and ability as a quilter too.

Enjoy your journey!
Claudia

Two-Block Formulas

What makes two blocks work well together to create an exciting quilt? It is easy to see that two blocks of the same size will fit together, and if each of those blocks has the same number of divisions, they might fit nicely side by side in a quilt. For instance, a nine-patch block will fit beside another nine-patch block, and a five-patch block will fit beside a five-patch block.

If two blocks can be made with the same measurements, they will fit side by side. The two five-patches can both be finished as a 10" or a 15" block, while the nine-patches can both finish as 9" blocks. That also means that a four-patch block can be placed beside a nine-patch if they are both 12" blocks.

After finding two blocks of the same dimensions, we simply place them side-by-side, alternating one block with another to make our quilt top. It usually looks best to have blocks which are alike in the corners of the quilt, so the number of blocks in each row is odd. In other words, your quilt top might have five blocks across and seven blocks down, or three blocks across and three blocks down. But, before combining these blocks of like dimensions, let's see if they complement one another

Will the pieces of one block appear to continue their design into the pieces of the next block? Will the pieces of the two blocks combine to form a secondary pattern? Will the pieces of one block seem to fit snugly into a space that was made perfectly for them in the next block? Does something exciting happen when two blocks are placed side by side, or does the combination appear flat and uninteresting? Do the blocks compete for attention or allow a unique design to appear? The right answers to all of these questions will determine if the secondary pattern will pop out and add a dramatic dimension to your quilt. Here are a few ideas that will help to make sure that happens.

Adding a Stepping-Stone Block

If we are simply looking for a block of the same dimensions and aren't worried about design lines, we might try adding a stepping-stone block. To design a stepping-stone block to fit next to your primary block, we divide a square of similar block dimensions into its primary square units. For example, a four-patch block will divide into four basic units across and down, while a five-patch block will divide into five basic units. Then, we can shade in the squares to radiate out from the center.

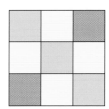

Nine-patch

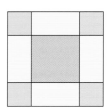

Four-patch

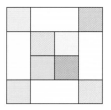

Four-patch

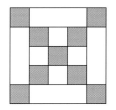

Five-patch

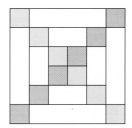

Six-patch

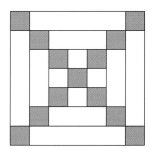

Seven-patch

Adding a Snowball-type Block

Another simple block that we can use as a secondary block is the Snowball. We can join a snowball-type block with almost any other block and a large star will be formed to surround the primary blocks. We design a Snowball block in much the same way as we did the stepping stone-type block. First we divide the block into its basic units. Then we draw a diagonal line across the corners of the block.

The color of the Snowball triangle must be darker than the neighboring colors so the large star will show up. I used snowball-type blocks to make Shoo Box, page 43, and Neighbor Girl, page 33.

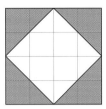

Four-patch

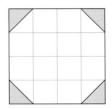

Four-patch

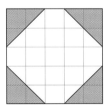

Five-patch

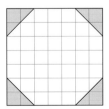

Seven-patch

Creating Secondary Patterns

Continuity of Lines

An exciting secondary pattern will appear when the two combined blocks complement each other and appear to connect. In order for two blocks to look connected, their lines must somehow flow in the same direction or appear to join.

Let's experiment with several 12" blocks that we could use together and then study the flow of the lines that they create. We will look at the way the block pieces interact and fit together. Then we will play with color changes to make the secondary patterns stand out.

First, we'll look at what appears when we combine Lone Star blocks with Mosaic variation blocks. Since Lone Star has two outward pointing triangles on each side, it's a good place to add blocks with lines that would flow toward the center of the star points. When we place a Mosaic variation beside Lone Star, a secondary pattern appears. Matching the fabric of adjoining pieces helps create a square that is on-point.

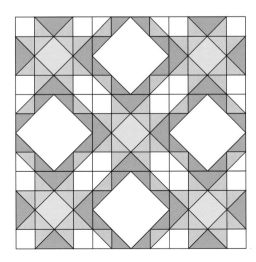

Similarly, the triangles of the Corn and Beans block fit into the side of Gentleman's Fancy, forming a gold and green box-like frame around the Corn and Beans block.

Like the Lone Star block, the Memories block has triangles that point outward. This time, however, the number of points and lines are doubled. When we place a Churn Dash variation block next to it, its lines continue the lines started by the Memories triangles. By matching the fabrics of the triangles whose points touch, we create a secondary design. The lines seem continuous even though the bright triangles are separated from each other.

Allowing The Secondary Design to Dominate

Sometimes we must choose one block as the primary focus to highlight the secondary pattern. I applied this principle to Wild Asters, page 97, and Tippecanoe Mosaic, page 91. In both cases, I wanted the more complex, star-type block to dominate. To make this happen, I muted the colors of the adjoining blocks except for the pieces that helped to make the secondary pattern, which I left darker.

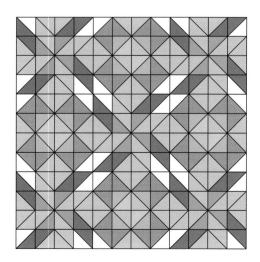

Turning Negatives into Positives

It may be necessary to change the traditional shades of a block to create a secondary pattern. When we change the background color from a light fabric to a dark fabric, we change a negative space to a positive one and the secondary pattern appears. This technique was used to make Kansas Windmill, page 54, and Eight-Point Puzzle, page 26. In both combinations we can see a crown-type star between the blocks when the negative spaces were changed to positive spaces.

Completer Borders

When the secondary design of a two-block quilt becomes the primary quilt design, continuing that design into the borders adds an impressive finishing touch. These borders usually make the design look complete so I call them Completer Borders. When we make a pieced completer border, we can usually copy elements found in the blocks since they automatically complement each other. After adding the pieced border, finish the quilt with a binding, or add a traditional strip-type border to the pieced border.

Following this design idea, I used elements from the Aircastle block to add a completer border to Castle Weather, page 14.

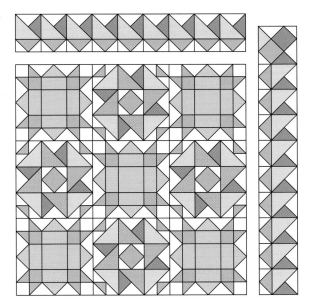

Churn Dash Memories, page 76, has broken, turquoise squares for its secondary design. The squares need to continue into the borders to look finished. The completer border is made of elements from both blocks to accentuate the lines of the blocks.

When blocks combine to form secondary stars, it is pleasing to continue those stars into the borders. In Eight-Point Puzzle, page 26, elements of the Eight-Point All Over block were repeated in the completer border to finish the red stars. Then new triangles were added to form yet another green star.

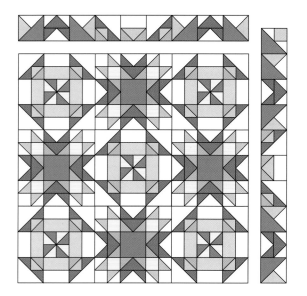 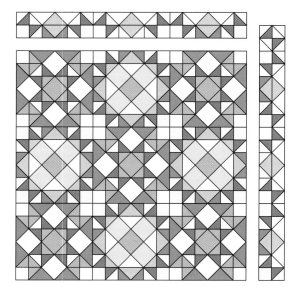

ow that we've gone over a few design principles, you're ready to have fun doing some experimenting of your own. Try combining some of your own favorite blocks with these design tips in mind and see what secondary designs will magically appear! Try new shades of colors in different parts of the block, more contrast or less contrast or look through books to find unusual block ideas to combine. Or use these ideas to select just the right fabric for making one of the exciting quilts in the book. Either way, the results are sure to be outstanding.

Two-Block Quilts

Enjoy this collection of wonderful two-block quilts. Each of them has that special sparkle that makes a quilt truly unique. The favorite traditional blocks combine to create dramatic patterns that give the quilts wonderful eye-catching appeal. You will undoubtedly recognize some of these old-favorite blocks, but you'll be amazed at just how they work together to form those exciting new secondary patterns.

For each of the delightful quilts you will find a helpful cutting chart and tips such as selecting your fabric to make the most of the secondary design or pointers on how that design comes together. Choose your favorite project and delight in unlocking the secrets of secondary patterns as you create a lovely two-block quilt.

Castle Weather

Finished size: 74" x 74"

Blocks: Weathervane and Aircastle

When the two blocks are placed next to one another, their lines create a zigzag pattern and the shapes appear to fit like puzzle pieces.

Materials: 42"-wide fabric

White (includes binding)	4¼ yards
Light navy	1⅝ yards
Medium teal	1 yard
Medium purple	⅓ yard
Light multicolor	1¼ yards
Dark navy	1 yard
Dark teal	⅝ yard
Backing	4½ yards
Batting	78" x 78"

Cut the following 42"-long strips and pieces. Cutting sizes are given in inches.

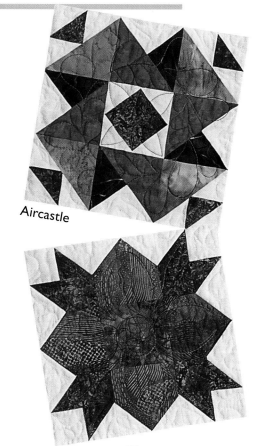

Aircastle

Weathervane

CUTTING CHART

Fabric	Number of strips	Size	First Cut Number	First Cut Size	Second Cut
WEATHERVANE BLOCK			Finished size: 12"		Make 13
White	4	2⅞	52	2⅞ x 2⅞	
	10	2½	156	2½ x 2½	
Light navy	4	2⅞	52	2⅞ x 2⅞	
	4	2½	52	2½ x 2½	
Medium teal	7	4½	52	4½ x 4½	
Medium purple	2	4½	13	4½ x 4½	
AIRCASTLE BLOCK			Finished size 12"		Make 12
White	6	2⅞	72	2⅞ x 2⅞	48 diagonally once
	2	5¼	12	5¼ x 5¼	
	3	2½	48	2½ x 2½	
Light navy	2	2⅞	24	2⅞ x 2⅞	
	2	4½	12	4½ x 4½	
Light multicolor	3	4⅞	24	4⅞ x 4⅞	diagonally once

Fabric	Number of strips	Size	First Cut Number	First Cut Size	Second Cut
AIRCASTLE BLOCK			Finished size 12"		Make 12
Dark navy	2	5¼	12	5¼ x 5¼	
Dark teal	3	4⅞	24	4⅞ x 4⅞	diagonally once
Pieced border					
White	1	2⅞	4	2⅞ x 2⅞	diagonally once
	8	2½	120	2½ x 2½	
	3	5¼	17	5¼ x 5¼	
Light navy	4	4½	60	2½ x 4½	
	1	3⁵⁄₁₆	4	3⁵⁄₁₆ x 3⁵⁄₁₆	
Light multicolor	4	4⅞	30	4⅞ x 4⅞	diagonally once
	1	5¼	1	5¼ x 5¼	
Dark navy	3	5¼	16	5¼ x 5¼	
	1	3⁵⁄₁₆	4	3⁵⁄₁₆ x 3⁵⁄₁₆	
Outside border and binding					
White (border)	8	1½			
(binding)	8	2¼			

Press carefully after each step, following the direction of the pressing arrows.

Weathervane Block

1. Refer to "Half-Square Triangles," page 105, and position a 2⅞" white square on a 2⅞" light navy square. Stitch, cut, and press. Make four to create eight half-square triangle units.

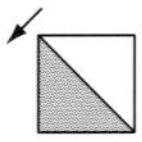

2. Sew one unit from step 1 to a 2½" light navy square as shown. Make four.

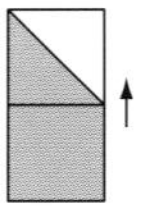

3. Sew one unit from step 1 to a 2½" white square as shown. Make four.

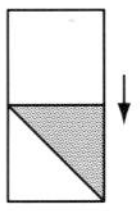

4. Sew one unit from step 2 and one unit from step 3 together as shown. Repeat to make a total of four.

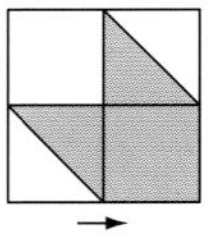

5. Refer to "Quick-Corner Triangles," page 106, and position a 2½" white square on the upper left corner of a 4½" medium teal square. Stitch to make a triangle corner. Press and trim. Repeat

to make a triangle on the upper right corner. Make a total of four.

6. Sew one unit from step 5 between two units from step 4. Make two.

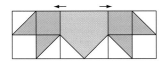

7. Sew two units from step 5 and one 4½" purple square together as shown.

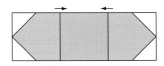

8. Sew the three sections together as shown to make the block.

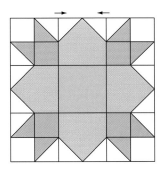

9. Repeat steps 1–8 to make a total of thirteen Weathervane blocks.

Aircastle Block

1. Refer to "Half-Square Triangles," page 105, and position a 2⅞" white square on a 2⅞" light navy square and stitch.

Cut and press. Make two to create four half square triangle units.

2. With right sides together, sew a small white triangle on adjacent sides of the light navy triangle as shown. Make four.

3. Sew one unit from step 2 to a light multi-color triangle as shown. Make four.

4. Refer to "Directional Triangles," page 105, and position a 5¼" white square on a 5¼" dark navy square. Stitch to the right of the drawn line so dark navy is on the right. Cut and press.

5. Sew one unit from step 4 to a dark teal triangle as shown and press. Repeat to make four.

6. Refer to "Quick-Corner Triangles," page 106, and position two 2½" white squares on opposite corners of a 4½" light navy square. Stitch to make a triangle corner. Press. Repeat on the remaining corners.

7. Sew one unit from step 5 between two units from step 3. Make two.

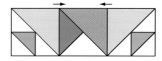

8. Sew the unit from step 6 between two units from step 5.

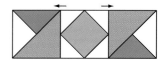

9. Sew the three sections together as shown to complete the block.

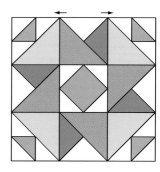

10. Repeat steps 1–9 to make a total of twelve Aircastle blocks.

Assembly

Refer to the quilt layout on page 19. Beginning with a Weathervane Block and alternating with the Aircastle blocks, lay out and sew the quilt in five rows with five blocks in each.

Pieced Border

1. Refer to "Quick-Corner Triangles," page 106, and position a 2½" white square on a 2½" x 4½" light navy rectangle. Stitch to make a triangle corner. Press and trim. Repeat to make a triangle on the opposite corner. Make sixty.

2. Refer to "Directional Triangles," page 105, and position a 5¼" white square on a 5¼" dark navy square. Stitch to the right of the drawn line so dark navy is on the right. Cut and press. Make fifteen to create sixty.

3. Sew one unit from step 2 to a multi-color triangle as shown and press. Repeat to make sixty.

4. Sew a unit from step 1 to a unit from step 3 as shown. Repeat to make sixty units, alternating pressing.

5. Sew fifteen of the units from step 4 together to create a border strip as shown in the quilt layout. Repeat to make four border strips.

6. As in step 2, position a 5¼" white square on a 5¼" dark navy square. Stitch to the right of the drawn line so dark navy is on the right. Cut and press. Make one to create four.

7. As in step 6, position a white square on a light multi-color square. Stitch to the left of the drawn line so the white will be on the right. Make one to create four.

8. Stitch a 3⁵⁄₁₆" light navy square to a 3⁵⁄₁₆" dark navy square. Add the small white triangles. Make four.

9. Using the units created in steps 6, 7, and 8, make four corner squares as shown.

10. Sew two borders to the top and bottom of the quilt.

11. Add a corner square to both ends of the two remaining border strips and sew to the sides of the quilt. Press.

Finishing

1. Referring to "Adding the Borders," page 106, add the 1½"-wide white borders to the quilt.

2. Referring to "Finishing the Quilt," page 108, layer, baste, and quilt as desired. Add binding to the quilt.

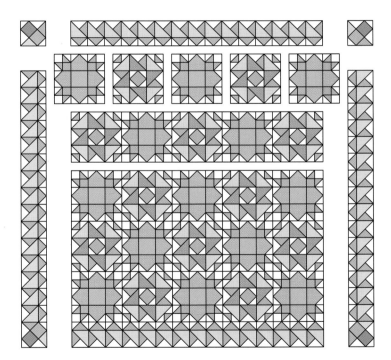

Rolling Rosebuds

Finished size: 72" x 72"

Blocks: Rolling Pinwheel and Rosebud

Choose a bold color for the Rosebud block since it plays such a dominant role and captures our attention. The dark blue and purple triangles in the corners of the blocks form a strong diagonal connection.

Materials: 42"-wide fabric

White	3¾ yards
Blue (includes binding)	2⅛ yards
Lavender	¾ yard
Floral print	1¼ yards
Purple	¼ yard
Red	1⅛ yards
Backing	4¼ yards
Batting	76" x 76"

Cut the following 42"-long strips and pieces. Cutting sizes are given in inches.

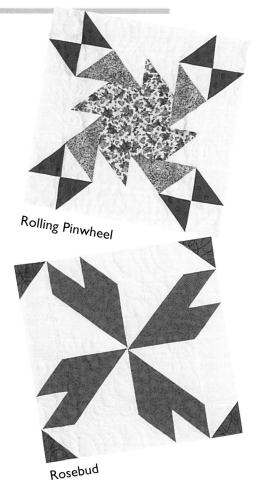

Rolling Pinwheel

Rosebud

CUTTING CHART

Fabric	Number of strips	Size	First Cut Number	First Cut Size
ROLLING PINWHEEL BLOCK		Finished size: 12"	Make 13	
White	4	2⅞	52	2⅞ x 2⅞
	4	4½	52	2½ x 4½
	13	2½	208	2½ x 2½
Blue	4	2⅞	52	2⅞ x 2⅞
Lavender	4	4½	52	2½ x 4½
Floral print	4	4½	52	2½ x 4½
ROSEBUD BLOCK		Finished size 12"	Make 12	
White	6	2⅞	72	2⅞ x 2⅞
	3	4⅞	24	4⅞ x 4⅞
	3	4½	48	2½ x 4½
Purple	2	2⅞	24	2⅞ x 2⅞
Red	4	2⅞	48	2⅞ x 2⅞
	3	4⅞	24	4⅞ x 4⅞

Fabric	Number of strips	Size	First Cut	
			Number	Size
Pieced borders				
White	8	2½	124	2½ x 2½
Blue	2	2⅞	24	2⅞ x 2⅞
	3	4½	40	2½ x 4½
Lavender	1	4½	16	2½ x 4½
Floral print	2	2⅞	24	2⅞ x 2⅞
	6	2½	84	2½ x 2½
Red	2	4½	24	2½ x 4½
Outside border and binding				
Blue (border)	8	2½		
(binding)	8	2¼		

Press carefully after each step, following the direction of the pressing arrows.

Rolling Pinwheel Block

1. Refer to "Half-Square Triangles," page 105, and position a 2⅞" white square on a 2⅞" blue square. Stitch, cut, and press. Make four to create eight half-square triangle units.

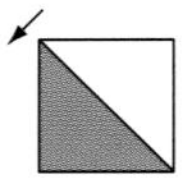

2. Sew a unit from step 1 to each end of a 2½" x 4½" white rectangle as shown. Make four.

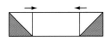

3. Refer to "Quick-Corner Triangles," page 106, and position a 2½" white square on a 2½" x 4½" lavender rectangle. Stitch to make a triangle corner. Press and trim. Repeat to make a triangle on the opposite end. Make four.

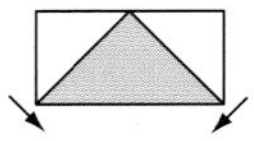

4. As in step 3, position a 2½" white square on the end of a 2½" x 4½" floral print rectangle as shown. Stitch to make a triangle corner. Repeat to make a total of four.

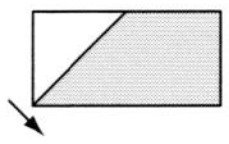

5. Sew the units from steps 3 and 4 together in pairs as shown. Make four.

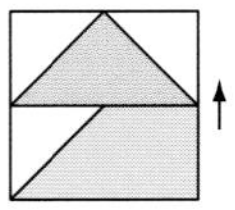

6. Sew the pairs from step 5 together as shown. Press.

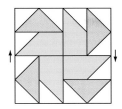

7. Sew two of the units from step 2 to the sides of the unit from step 6.

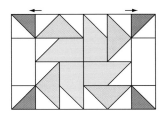

8. Add a 2½" white square to each end of the remaining units from step 2 and sew them to the top and bottom to complete the block.

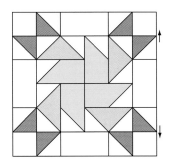

9. Repeat steps 1–8 to make a total of thirteen Rolling Pinwheel blocks.

Rosebud Block

1. Refer to "Half-Square Triangles," page 105, and position a white 2⅞" square on a purple 2⅞" square and stitch. Cut and press. Make two to create four half-square triangle units.

2. Repeat step 1 using white and red 2⅞" squares. Make four to create eight half-square triangle units.

3. Repeat step 1 using 4⅞" white and red squares. Make two to create four half-square triangle units.

4. Assemble the four units from step 3 as shown.

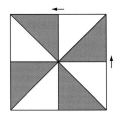

5. Sew the units from step 2 into pairs as shown. Make four.

6. Attach a 2½" x 4½" white rectangle to the right side of each of the units from step 5. Make four.

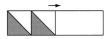

7. Sew a unit from step 6 to the sides of the center unit from step 4.

8. Add a purple triangle unit from step 1 to each end of the remaining units from step 6. Sew to the top and bottom to complete the block.

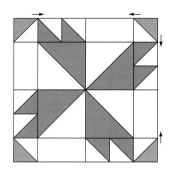

9. Repeat steps 1–8 to make a total of twelve Rosebud blocks.

Assembly

Refer to the quilt layout on page 25. Beginning with a Rosebud block and alternating with the Rolling Pinwheel blocks, lay out and sew the quilt in five rows with five blocks in each.

Pieced Border

1. Refer to "Half-Square Triangles," page 105, and position a 2⅞" blue square on top of a 2⅞" floral print square and stitch. Cut and press. Make twenty-four to create forty-eight half-square triangle units.

2. Sew a 2½" white square to the end of the units from step 1 as shown to make a total of twenty. Rotate the triangle unit and add a white square as shown to make a total of twenty. Set aside.

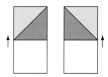

3. Refer to "Quick-Corner Triangles," page 106, and position a 2½" floral print square on one end of a 2½" x 4½" red rectangle. Stitch to make a triangle corner. Repeat to make a white triangle on the opposite end. Make twelve.

4. Repeat step 3 but reverse the white and floral squares to make 12 mirror-image triangle units. Set aside.

5. To make blue triangle units, repeat step 2 using 2½" x 4½" blue rectangles, 2½" white squares, and 2½" floral print squares to make a total of twenty blue triangle units. Set aside.

6. Repeat step 5, reversing the white and floral print squares to make twenty mirror-image blue triangle units. Set aside.

7. To make lavender triangle units, repeat step 3, using 2½" x 4½" lavender rectangles, 2½" white squares, and 2½" floral print squares. Make a total of eight and set aside.

8. Repeat step 7, reversing the floral print and blue squares to make eight mirror-image lavender triangle units. Set aside.

9. To make corner squares, sew together two triangle units from step 1, a 2½" floral print square, and a 2½" white square as shown. Make four.

10. To make red triangle border sections, sew together the units from above as shown. Make twelve.

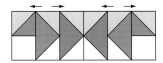

11. To make lavender triangle border sections, sew together the units from above as shown. Make eight.

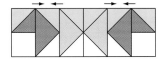

12. Beginning with a red triangle border section and alternating with the lavender triangle border sections, lay out and sew the borders in four rows with five units in each.

13. Sew border strips to the sides and press. Sew two corner squares to the ends of the remaining border strips, positioning as shown. Sew to the top and bottom of the quilt.

Finishing

1. Referring to "Adding the Borders," page 106, add the 2½"-wide blue borders to the quilt.

2. Referring to "Finishing the Quilt," page 108, layer, baste, and quilt as desired. Add the binding to the quilt.

Eight-Point Puzzle

Finished size: 70" x 70"

Blocks: Indian Puzzle Variation and Eight-Point All Over

The Indian Puzzle variation blocks are meant to be dominant so choose darker, more vibrant colors for them. The Eight-Point All Over block is meant to be more recessive. A green secondary star pattern is created in the pieced borders.

Materials: 42"-wide fabric

Dark green	1¼ yards
Lavender/green	½ yard
Light beige	2⅓ yards
Floral print (includes binding)	2½ yards
Rose	1 yard
Light green	½ yard
Lavender	1 yard
Medium beige	⅝ yard
Backing	4¼ yards
Batting	74" x 74"

Cut the following 42"-long strips and pieces.
Cutting sizes are given in inches.

Indian Puzzle variation

Eight-Point All Over

CUTTING CHART

Fabric	Number of strips	Size	First Cut Number	First Cut Size	Second Cut
INDIAN PUZZLE VARIATION BLOCK			Finished size: 10½"		Make 13
Dark green	4	3¾	26	3¾ x 3¾	
Lavender/green	2	3¾	13	3¾ x 3¾	
Light beige	2	3¾	13	3¾ x 3¾	
	4	3	52	3 x 3	
	3	2¼	52	2¼ x 2¼	
Floral print	1	3	13	3 x 3	
	2	2⅝	26	2⅝ x 2⅝	diagonally once
	2	4¾	13	4¾ x 4¾	
Rose	2	4¾	26	4¾ x 4¾	13 diagonally twice

Fabric	Number of strips	Size	First Cut		Second Cut
			Number	Size	
EIGHT-POINT ALL OVER BLOCK			Finished size 10½"	Make 12	
Dark green	4	2⅝	48	2⅝ x 2⅝	
Light beige	4	2⅝	48	2⅝ x 2⅝	
	2	4¾	12	4¾ x 4¾	diagonally twice
Floral print	1	3	12	3 x 3	
Rose	5	2¼	80	2¼ x 2¼	
Light green	3	4	48	2¼ x 4	
	2	2⅝	24	2⅝ x 2⅝	diagonally once
Lavender	4	3	48	3 x 3	
Medium beige	4	2¼	64	2¼ x 2¼	
Pieced border					
Dark green	3	2⅝	44	2⅝ x 2⅝	
Light beige	3	2⅝	44	2⅝ x 2⅝	
	4	2¼	64	2¼ x 2¼	
	3	2¼	40	2¼ x 2¼	
Rose	2	2¼	24	2¼ x 2¼	
Light green	2	4	20	4 x 4	
Medium beige	2	2¼	24	2¼ x 2¼	
	1	2¼	16	2¼ x 2¼	
Outside borders and binding					
Lavender (border)	8	2¼			
Floral print (border)	8	4			
(binding)	8	2¼			

Press carefully after each step, following the direction of the pressing arrows.

Indian Puzzle Variation Block

1. Refer to "Directional Triangles," page 105, and position a 3¾" lavender/green square on a 3¾" dark green square and a 3¾" light beige on a 3¾" dark green square. Stitch to the left of the drawn line so the dark green is always on the left. Cut and press the pairs. Make one of each to create four triangle units of each.

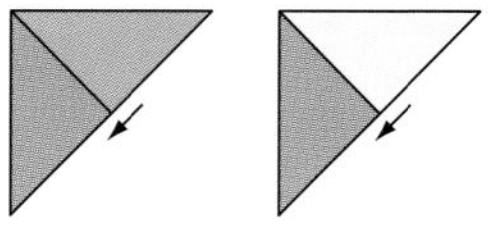

2. Sew the triangles from step 1 together as shown. Trim to 3" x 3" if necessary. Make four.

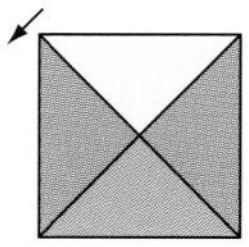

3. Sew a unit from step 2 to each side of the 3" floral print center square.

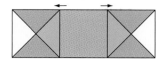

4. Sew a 3" light beige square to each side of both the remaining units from step 2.

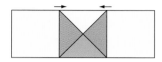

5. Sew the two units from step 4 to the unit from step 3.

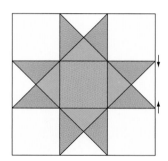

6. Repeat step 1 using a 4¾" floral print square on a 4¾" rose square. Stitch to the left of the drawn line, cut, and press.

7. Sew a small floral print triangle to a 2¼" light beige square, as shown. Make four.

8. Sew a rose triangle to the unit from step 7 as shown. Make four.

9. Sew the units from step 8 to the units from step 6 as shown. Make four.

10. Sew the units from step 9 to the sides of the unit from step 5 as shown to complete the block.

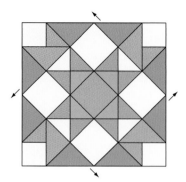

11. Repeat steps 1–10 to make a total of thirteen Indian Puzzle variation blocks.

Eight-Point All Over Block

1. Refer to "Half-Square Triangles," page 105, and position a 2⅝" light beige square on a 2⅝" dark green square. Stitch, cut, and press. Make four to create eight half-square triangles.

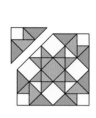

2. Refer to "Quick-Corner Triangles," page 106, and position a 2¼" rose square on 2¼" x 4" light green rectangle. Stitch to make a triangle corner. Press. Repeat to make a triangle on the opposite end. Make four.

3. Sew a 3" lavender square to each side of the 3" floral print center square. Make one.

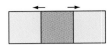

4. Sew a light beige triangle to opposite sides of a lavender square. Make two.

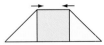

5. Sew the units from step 4 to each side of the center unit from step 3.

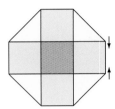

6. Sew the small light green triangles to the corners of the unit from step 5 as shown.

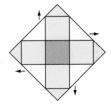

7. Sew a unit from step 1 to each side of the unit from step 2 as shown.

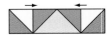

8. Sew two of the units from step 7 to the sides of the unit from step 6.

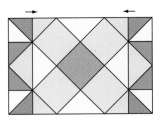

9. Sew a medium beige 2¼" square to each end of the remaining two units from step 7 as shown.

10. Attach the units from step 9 to the top and bottom of the unit from step 8 to complete the block.

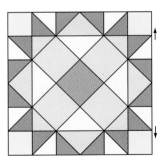

11. Repeat steps 1–10 to make a total of four interior Eight-Point All Over blocks.

12. To make the exterior Eight-Point All Over blocks, repeat steps 1–10, but make three of step 2 as instructed, and

one using medium beige squares on a light green rectangle. Make eight.

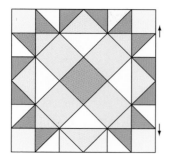

Assembly

Refer to the quilt layout on page 32. Beginning with an Indian Puzzle variation block and alternating with the Eight-Point All Over blocks, lay out and sew the quilt in five rows with five blocks in each. Place the eight exterior Eight-Point All Over blocks around the outside of the quilt top with the beige/floral print side facing outward.

Pieced Border

1. Refer to "Half-Square Triangles," page 105, using 2⅝" light beige and dark green squares. Stitch, cut, and press. Make forty-four to create eighty-eight half-square triangle units.

2. Using two of the units from step 1, one 2¼" medium beige square, and one 2¼" light beige square, assemble as shown. Make twenty-four.

3. Using two of the units from step 1 and two 2¼" light beige squares, assemble as shown. Make sixteen.

4. Refer to "Quick-Corner Triangles," page 106, and position a 2¼" rose square on two corners of a 4" light green square. Stitch to make triangle corners. Press and trim. Repeat to make light beige triangles on the two remaining corners. Make twelve.

5. Repeat step 4, positioning a 2¼" medium beige square onto two corners of a 4" light green square and light beige triangles on the remaining corners. Make eight.

6. Sew two of the units from step 2 to one of the units from step 4 as shown. Make twelve.

   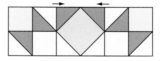

7. Sew two of the units from step 3 to one of the units from step 5 as shown. Make eight.

8. Using two units from step 1 and two 2¼" light beige squares, assemble the corner square as shown. Make four.

9. Beginning with a border unit from step 6 and alternating with the border unit from step 7, lay out and sew the borders in four rows with five border units in each.

10. Sew one border from step 9 to each side of the quilt.

11. Sew one corner square from step 8 to each end of the two remaining borders. Sew the borders to the top and bottom of the quilt.

Finishing

1. Referring to "Adding the Borders," page 106, add the 2¼"-wide lavender print borders and the 4¼"-wide floral print border to the quilt.

2. Referring to "Finishing the Quilt," page 108, layer and quilt as desired. Add binding to the quilt.

Neighbor Girl

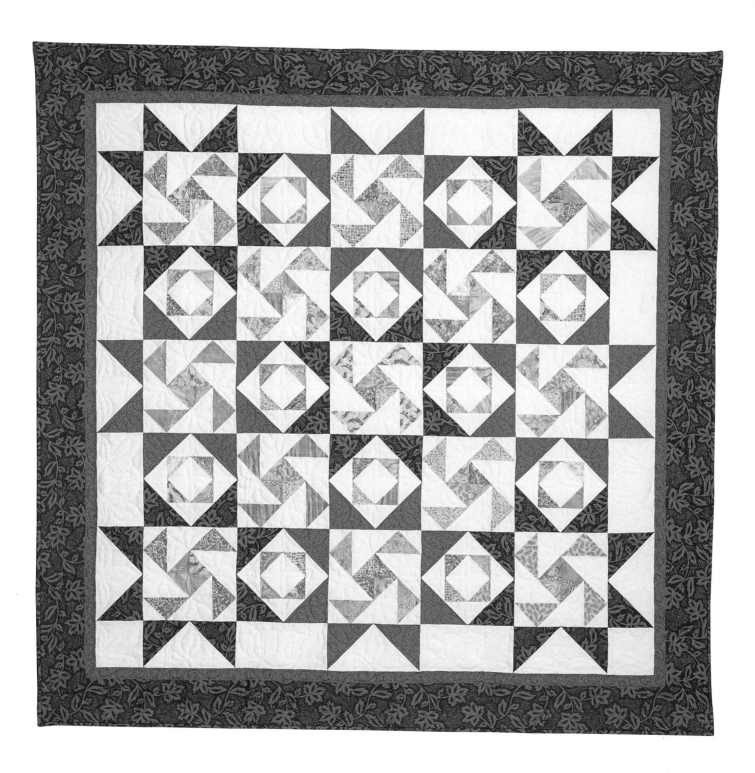

Neighbor Girl

Finished size: 58" x 58"

Blocks: Next Door Neighbor and Diamond Girl

By using a dark fabric in the large corner triangles of Diamond Girl, you will create a secondary star pattern. The large border triangles will complete the star.

Materials: 42"-wide fabric

White print	2½ yards
Assorted medium blue prints	⅝ yard
Assorted medium green prints	⅝ yard
Royal blue print (includes binding)	2¼ yards
Teal print	¾ yard
Backing	3½ yards
Batting	62" x 62"

Next Door Neighbor

Diamond Girl

Cut the following 42"-long strips and pieces. Cutting sizes are given in inches.

CUTTING CHART

Fabric	Number of strips	Size	First Cut Number	First Cut Size	Second Cut
NEXT DOOR NEIGHBOR BLOCK			Finished size: 8"		Make 13
White	7	2½	104	2½ x 2½	
	4	4½	52	2½ x 4½	
Med. Blues	2	4½	26	2½ x 4½	
	2	2½	26	2½ x 2½	
Med. Greens	2	4½	26	2½ x 4½	
	2	2½	26	2½ x 2½	
DIAMOND GIRL BLOCK			Finished size 8"		Make 12
Royal Blue	2	4⅞	12	4⅞ x 4⅞	diagonally once
White	2	4½	12	4½ x 4½	
	3	3⅞	24	3⅞ x 3⅞	diagonally once
Teal	2	4⅞	12	4⅞ x 4⅞	diagonally once
Med. Blues	2	2½	24	2½ x 2½	
Med. Greens	2	2½	24	2½ x 2½	

Fabric	Number of strips	Size	First Cut		Second Cut
			Number	Size	
Pieced border					
Royal Blue	2	4½	16	4½ x 4½	
White	3	8½	20	4½ x 8½	
	1	4½	4	4½ x 4½	
Teal	1	4½	8	4½ x 4½	
Outside borders and binding					
Royal Blue (border)	8	4½			
(binding)	7	2¼			
Teal (border)	6	1½			

Press carefully after each step, following the direction of the pressing arrows.

Next Door Neighbor Block

1. Refer to "Quick-Corner Triangles," page 106, and position a 2½" white square on a 2½" x 4½" medium blue or medium green piece. Stitch to make a triangle corner. Press. Repeat to make a triangle on the opposite end. Make four using an assortment of blues and greens.

2. As in step 1, position a 2½" medium blue or green square on the end of a 2½" x 4½" white piece as shown. Stitch to make a triangle corner. Repeat to make a total of four.

3. Sew one unit from step 1 and one unit from step 2 together as shown and press. Repeat to make four pairs.

4. Sew four pairs from step 3 together as shown to complete the block.

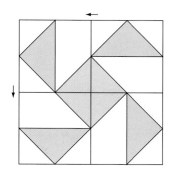

5. Repeat steps 1–4 to make a total of thirteen Next Door Neighbor blocks.

Diamond Girl Block

1. With right sides together sew a 2½" blue or green square on 4½" white square. Stitch to make a triangle corner. Repeat to make a triangle in all four corners.

2. Sew the white triangles to the sides of the square from step 2. Square up the block so it measures 5⅝", if necessary.

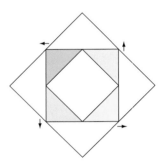

3. Repeat step 2 to sew a royal blue triangle on one side of the block from step 3, and a teal triangle on the opposite side. Then add one royal blue and one teal triangle to the remaining sides.

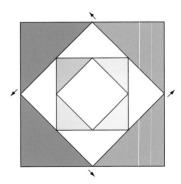

4. Repeat steps 1–3 to make a total of twelve Diamond Girl blocks.

Assembly

Refer to the quilt layout on page 37. Beginning with a Next Door Neighbor block and alternating with the Diamond Girl blocks, lay out and sew the quilt in five rows with five blocks in each.

Pieced Border

1. Refer to "Quick-Corner Triangles," page 106, and position one 4½" royal blue square on a 4½" x 8½" white rectangle. Stitch to make a triangle corner. Repeat to add a royal blue triangle on the opposite end.

2. Repeat step 1 to make a total of eight royal blue and white units and four teal and white units.

> **U**se the triangles trimmed from step 1, and you have a head start on another project! After stitching, trim both the white and blue or teal triangles. Square them up and sew together to make half-square triangles. A great beginning for a baby quilt!

3. Sew together two royal blue units, one teal unit, and two 4½" x 8½" white rectangles as shown in the quilt layout, page 37. Repeat to make four border strips. Sew one strip to the sides of the quilt and press.

4. Sew a 4½" white square to each end of the two remaining triangle border strips. Press. Sew these strips to the top and bottom and press.

Finishing

1. Referring to "Adding the Borders," page 106, add the 1½"-wide teal border and the 4½"-wide royal blue border to the quilt.

2. Referring to "Finishing the Quilt," page 108, layer and quilt as desired. Add binding to the quilt.

Fancy Corn and Beans

Finished Size: 74" x 98"

Blocks: Corn and Beans and Gentleman's Fancy

The Corn and Beans blocks appear to be set on point, since their gold color continues into the Gentleman's Fancy blocks. The center of the Gentleman's Fancy blocks is simplified to make room for a large print.

Materials: 42"-wide fabric

Beige	2⅝ yards
Green	1¼ yards
Red	½ yard
Gold	1¼ yards
Brown	1⅜ yards
Large print	2⅝ yards
Yellow-green	½ yard
Olive green (includes binding)	2 yards
Backing	5¾ yards
Batting	78" x 102"

Gentleman's Fancy

Corn and Beans

Cut the following strips and pieces. Cutting sizes are given in inches.

CUTTING CHART

Fabric	Number of strips	Size	First Cut Number	First Cut Size	Second Cut
CORN AND BEANS BLOCK			Finished size: 12"		Make 18
Beige	9	2⅞	108	2⅞ x 2⅞	72 diagonally once
	7	4⅞	54	4⅞ x 4⅞	diagonally once
Green	9	2⅞	108	2⅞ x 2⅞	72 diagonally once
Red	3	4⅞	18	4⅞ x 4⅞	diagonally once
Gold	9	2½	144	2½ x 2½	
Brown	5	4½	72	2½ x 4½	
GENTLEMAN'S FANCY			Finished size 12"		Make 17
Beige	5	5¼	34	5¼ x 5¼	diagonally twice
Green	2	2½	17	2½ x 2½	
	2	4⅞	9	4⅞ x 4⅞	diagonally once

CUTTING CHART (continued)

Fabric	Number of strips	Size	First Cut Number	First Cut Size	Second Cut
GENTLEMAN'S FANCY (Continued)			Finished size 12"		Make 17
Yellow-green	2	2½	17	2½ x 2½	
	2	4⅞	9	4⅞ x 4⅞	diagonally once
Brown	2	2½	34	2½ x 2½	
	3	4⅞	17	4⅞ x 4⅞	diagonally once
Large print ✓	5	8½	17	8½ x 8½	
Gold *yellow*	3	5¼	17	5¼ x 5¼	diagonally twice
Outside borders and binding					
Olive green (border)	19	2			
(binding)	9	2¼			
Large print (border)	11	4½			

Press carefully after each step, following the direction of the pressing arrows.

Corn and Bean Blocks

1. Refer to "Half-Square Triangles," page 105, and position a 2⅞" beige square on a green 2⅞" square. Stitch, cut, and press. Make two to create four half-square triangle units.

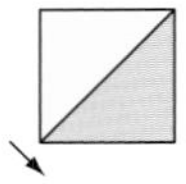

2. Sew small beige triangles on adjacent sides as shown. Make four.

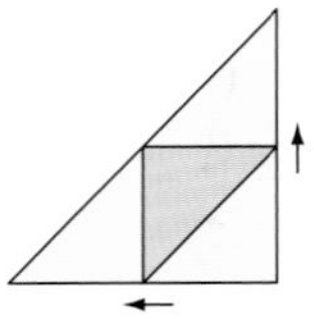

3. Sew a large red triangle to two of the units from step 2. Sew beige triangles to the remaining two units from step 2.

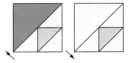

4. Sew the units from step 3 together as shown.

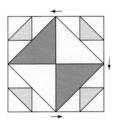

5. Refer to "Quick-Corner Triangles," page 106, and position a 2½" gold square on a 2½" x 4½" brown rectangle. Stitch to make a triangle corner. Press. Repeat to make a triangle on the opposite end. Make four.

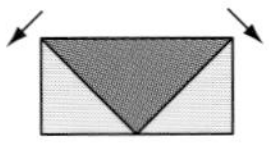

6. Sew a small green triangle onto each end of the units from step 5 as shown.

7. Sew the units from step 6 to the unit from step 3 as shown.

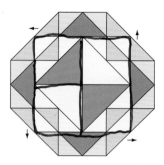

8. Add the large beige triangles to the corners to complete the block.

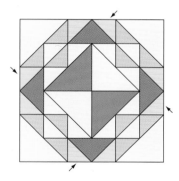

9. Repeat steps 1–8 to make a total of eighteen Corn and Beans blocks.

Gentleman's Fancy Block

1. Refer to "Quick-Corner Triangles," page 106, and position a 2½" green square on the corner of a 8½" large print square. Stitch to make a triangle corner. Press and trim. Repeat to make a yellow/green triangle on the lower right corner, and brown triangles on the upper right and lower left corners.

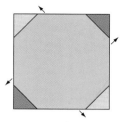

2. Sew one gold triangle and two beige triangles as shown. Make four.

3. Sew the units from step 2 to the sides of the unit from step 1.

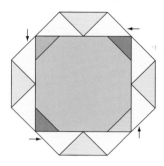

4. Sew the large triangles onto the corners, matching color to the nearest small triangle, to complete the block.

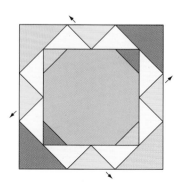

5. Repeat steps 1–4 to make a total of seventeen Gentleman's Fancy blocks.

Assembly

Refer to the quilt layout on page 42. Beginning with a Corn and Beans block and alternating with the Gentleman's Fancy blocks, lay out and sew the quilt in seven rows with five blocks in each.

Finishing

1. Referring to "Adding the Borders," page 107, add the 2"-wide inner and outer olive green borders and the 4½"-wide middle large print border to the quilt.

2. Referring to "Finishing the Quilt," page 108, layer and quilt as desired. Add binding to the quilt.

Shoo Box

Shoo Box

Shoo-Fly

Shadow Box

Finished size: 63" x 86"

Blocks: Shoo-Fly and Shadow Box

Since this quilt is set on point, it uses large pieced setting triangles along the sides and pieced corner triangles. Careful fabric selection will enable a large purple star to emerge as a secondary design.

Materials: 42"-wide fabric

Assorted beiges	3¾ yards
Green	1 yard
Red	⅞ yard
Purple (includes binding)	3 yards
Backing	5¼ yards
Batting	68" x 91"

Cut the following 42"-long strips and pieces.
Cutting sizes are given in inches.

CUTTING CHART

Fabric	Number of strips	Size	First Cut Number	First Cut Size	Second Cut
SHOO-FLY BLOCK			Finished size: 8"		Make 35
Beige	11	2⅞	140	2⅞ x 2⅞	
	9	4½	140	2½ x 4½	
Green	11	2⅞	140	2⅞ x 2⅞	
SHADOW BOX BLOCK			Finished size 8"		Make 24
Beige	3	4½	24	4½ x 4½	
	5	3¾	48	3¾ x 3¾	diagonally once
Red	6	2½	96	2½ x 2½	
Purple	6	4⅞	48	4⅞ x 4⅞	diagonally once
Setting triangles (Make 20) and Corner triangles (Make 4)					
Beige	1	3⅜	20	1⅞ x 3⅜	
	2	3¾	20	3¾ x 3¾	diagonally once
	1	3⅞	2	3⅞ x 3⅞	diagonally once
	1	2	4	2 x 2	
Red	1	2⅜	4	2⅜ x 2⅜	diagonally once
	1	2⅞	10	2⅞ x 2⅞	diagonally once
	2	2¼	20	2¼ x 2¼	diagonally once

Fabric	Number of strips	Size	First Cut		Second Cut
			Number	Size	
Setting triangles (Make 20) and Corner triangles (Make 4) (Continued)					
Purple	2	3¾	20	3¾ x 3¾	diagonally once
	1	3⅞	4	3⅞ x 3⅞	diagonally once
	2	4⅞	10	4⅞ x 4⅞	diagonally once
Outside border and binding					
Purple (border)	9	3½			
(binding)	8	2¼			

Press carefully after each step, following the direction or the pressing arrows.

Shoo-Fly Block

1. Refer to "Half-Square Triangles," page 105, and position a 2⅞" green square on a 2⅞" beige square. Stitch, cut, and press. Make four to create eight half-square triangle units.

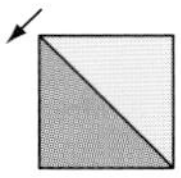

2. Sew four half-square triangles to create the center square as shown.

3. Sew a 4½" x 2½" beige rectangle to the sides of the unit from step 2.

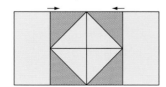

4. Sew a half square triangle from step 1 to each end of a 4½" x 2½" beige rectangle as shown. Make two. Sew to the top and bottom to complete the block.

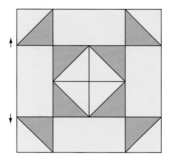

5. Repeat steps 1–4 to make a total of 35 Shoo-fly blocks.

Shadow Box Block

1. Refer to "Quick Corner Triangles," page 106, and position a 2½" red square on a 4½" beige square. Stitch to make a triangle corner. Repeat to make a triangle in all four corners.

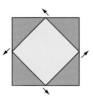

2. Sew small beige triangles to all four sides of the square from step 1.

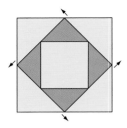

3. Repeat to sew large purple triangles to the sides of the square from step 3. Block will measure 8½" square.

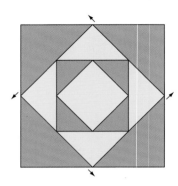

4. Repeat steps 1–3 to make a total of 24 Shadow Box blocks.

Setting Triangles

1. Sew a small 2¼" red triangle to each end of a 1⅞" x 3⅜" beige rectangle as shown.

2. Sew a large 2⅞" red triangle to the unit from step 1 as shown.

3. Sew large 3¾" beige triangles to the unit from step 2 as shown.

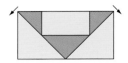

4. Sew one large 4⅞" and two small 3¾" purple triangles to the unit as shown.

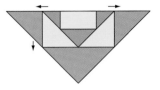

5. Repeat steps 1–4 to make a total of 20 setting triangles.

Corner Triangles

1. Sew two small 2⅜" red triangles to a 2" x 2" beige square as shown.

2. Sew a large 3⅞" beige triangle to the unit from step 1 as shown.

3. Sew the 3⅞" purple triangles to the unit from step 2 as shown.

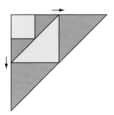

4. Repeat steps 1–3 to make a total of 4 corner triangles.

Assembly

Refer to the quilt layout below. Join Shoo-fly blocks to Shadow Box blocks in the alternating pattern shown to create diagonal rows. Attach setting triangles to the sides and corner triangles to corners. Join the rows.

Finishing

1. Referring to "Adding the Borders," page 106, add the 3½"-wide purple border to the quilt.

2. Referring to "Finishing the Quilt," page 108, layer and quilt as desired. Add bindings to the quilt.

Illinois Card Trick

Finished size: 41" x 41"

Blocks: Card Trick and Illinois

These two well-fitted blocks form secondary light squares where their corners meet. The design in completed out into the border by repeating elements found in the blocks.

Materials: 42"-wide fabric

Light Beige	1 ¼ yards
Red	½ yard
Green (includes binding)	1 ¼ yards
Dark Beige	¼ yard
Gold print	¼ yard
Orange	½ yard
Floral print	⅝ yard
Backing	2 ½ yards
Batting	45" x 45"

Cut the following 42"-long strips and pieces.
Cutting sizes are given in inches.

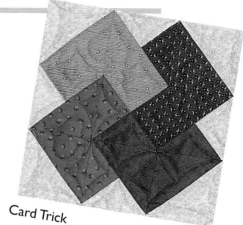

Card Trick

Illinois

CUTTING CHART

Fabric	Number of strips	Size	First Cut Number	First Cut Size	Second Cut
CARD TRICK BLOCK			Finished size: 9"		Make 5
Light Beige	1	4¼	5	4¼ x 4¼	diagonally twice
	1	3⅞	10	3⅞ x 3⅞	diagonally once
Red	1	4¼	3	4¼ x 4¼	diagonally twice
	from above 4¼ strip		5	3⅞ x 3⅞	diagonally once
Green	1	4¼	3	4¼ x 4¼	diagonally twice
	from above 4¼ strip		5	3⅞ x 3⅞	diagonally once
Dark Beige	1	4¼	3	4¼ x 4¼	diagonally twice
	from above 4¼ strip		5	3⅞ x 3⅞	diagonally once
Orange	1	4¼	3	4¼ x 4¼	diagonally twice
	from above 4¼ strip		5	3⅞ x 3⅞	diagonally once
ILLINOIS BLOCK			Finished size 9"		Make 4
Light Beige	4	2	64	2 x 2	
	1	3⅞	8	3⅞ x 3⅞	

Fabric	Number of strips	Size	First Cut		Second Cut
			Number	Size	
ILLINOIS BLOCK (Continued)		Finished size 9"		Make 4	
Red	1	3½	16	2 x 3½	
Green	1	2	16	2 x 2	
Gold print	1	3½	16	2 x 3½	
Floral print	1	3⅞	8	3⅞ x 3⅞	
	1	3½	4	3½ x 3½	
Pieced border					
Light Beige	2	2	32	2 x 2	
	2	3⅞	14	3⅞ x 3⅞	
	1	4¼	1	4¼ x 4¼	
Red	1	3½	8	2 x 3½	
Green	1	4¼	1	4¼ x 4¼	
	from above 4¼ strip		2	3⅞ x 3⅞	
Floral print	1	3½	8	2 x 3½	
	2	3⅞	14	3⅞ x 3⅞	2 diagonally once
Outside borders and binding					
Green (border)	5	3½			
(binding)	5	2¼			
Orange (border)	4	1½			

To avoid confusion while piecing, create a mock-up by pinning patches on a flannel board. Position the flannel board on the wall beside your sewing machine.

Press carefully after each step, following the direction of the pressing arrows.

Card Trick Block

1. With right sides together, join one small light beige triangle to one small red triangle. Repeat with light beige and

green, light beige and dark beige, and light beige and orange for a total of four units as shown.

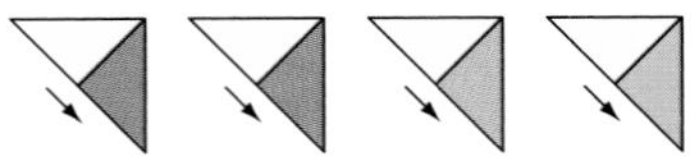

2. Sew a large dark beige triangle to the red/light beige unit from step 1, a large red triangle to the green/light beige unit, a large orange triangle to the dark beige/light beige unit, and a large green triangle to the orange/light beige unit.

3. Sew the center square using one small triangle each of dark beige, red, green, and orange as shown.

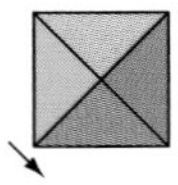

4. Sew a large light beige triangle to a large dark beige, red, green, and orange triangle.

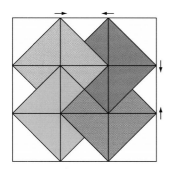

5. Sew the units together into three rows. Sew the rows together to make the block as shown.

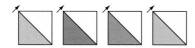

6. Repeat steps 1–5 to make a total of five Card Trick blocks.

Illinois Block

1. Refer to "Quick-Corner Triangles," page 106, and position a 2" light beige square on a 2" x 3½" red rectangle. Stitch to make a triangle corner. Press. Repeat to make a triangle on the opposite end. Make four.

2. Repeat step 1 using light beige squares and gold print rectangles. Make four.

3. Sew one unit from step 1 to one unit from step 2 as shown. Repeat to make four.

4. Refer to "Half-Square Triangles," page 105, and position a 3⅞" light beige square on top of a 3⅞" floral print square. Stitch, cut, and press. Make two

to create four half-square triangle units.

5. As in step 1, position a 2" green square on one corner of a 3½" floral print square. Stitch to make the triangle corner. Repeat to make a triangle on all four corners. Make one.

6. Sew the units together into rows and sew the three rows together to form the block.

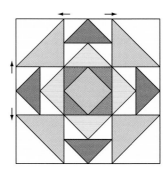

7. Repeat steps 1–6 to make a total of four Illinois blocks.

Assembly

Refer to the quilt layout on page 53. Beginning with a Card Trick block and alternating with the Illinois blocks, lay out and sew the quilt in three rows with three blocks in each.

Pieced Border

1. Refer to "Quick-Corner Triangles," page 106, and position a 2" light beige square on the end of a 2" x 3½" red rectangle. Stitch to make a triangle corner. Press. Repeat to make a triangle on the opposite end. Make eight.

2. Repeat step 1 using light beige squares and floral print rectangles. Make eight.

3. Sew one unit from step 1 to one unit from step 2 as shown. Repeat to make eight.

4. Refer to "Half-Square Triangles," page 105, and position a 3⅞" light beige square on a 3⅞" floral print square. Stitch, cut, and press. Make twelve to create twenty-four half-square triangle units.

5. Repeat step 4 using green and light beige squares. Make two to create four half-square triangle units.

6. Refer to "Directional Triangles," page 105, and position a 4¼" light beige square on a 4¼" green square. Stitch to the right of the line, cut, and press. Make one to create four directional triangles with the green on the right.

7. Sew a large floral print triangle to the green/light beige units from step 6. Make four.

8. Sew two half-square triangle units from step 4 to one unit from step 3 as shown. Repeat to make eight.

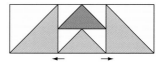

9. Sew half-square triangle units from steps 4 and 5 to one unit from step 7 as shown. Repeat to make four.

10. Sew two units from step 8 to one unit from step 9 as shown below. Repeat to make four border strips.

11. Sew two border strips to the sides of the quilt top.

12. Sew the remaining step 4 light biege/floral half-square triangle units to the ends of the remaining two border strips and sew to the top and bottom.

Finishing

1. Referring to "Adding the Borders," page 106, add the 1½"-wide orange borders and the 3½"-wide green borders to the quilt.

2. Referring to "Finishing the Quilt," page 108, layer, baste, and quilt as desired. Add binding to the quilt.

Kansas Windmill

Finished size: 64" x 64"

Blocks: Kansas and Windmill

When you join the Kansas and Windmill blocks, a secondary crown-type star appears. To make the secondary design dominant, choose a dark color like the royal blue used here.

Materials: 42"-wide fabric

White	2½ yards
Medium green	1⅝ yards
Light pink	⅜ yard
Light green	⅓ yard
Blue	2 yards
Bright pink (includes binding)	1½ yards
Backing	3⅞ yards
Batting	68" x 68"

Cut the following 42"-long strips and pieces. Cutting sizes are given in inches.

Windmill

Kansas

CUTTING CHART

Fabric	Number of strips	Size	First Cut Number	First Cut Size
KANSAS BLOCK		Finished size: 12"	Make 13	
White	7	2½	104	2½ x 2½
	4	4½	52	2½ x 4½
Medium green	4	4½	52	2½ x 4½
Bright pink	4	2½	52	2½ x 2½
	4	2⅞	52	2⅞ x 2⅞
Light green	2	4½	13	4½ x 4½
Blue	10	2½	156	2½ x 2½
	4	2⅞	52	2⅞ x 2⅞
WINDMILL BLOCK		Finished size 12"	Make 12	
White	6	4½	96	2½ x 4½
	6	2½	96	2½ x 2½
	2	2⅞	24	2⅞ x 2⅞

| Fabric | Number of strips | Size | First Cut | |
			Number	Size
WINDMILL BLOCK (Continued)		Finished size 12"	Make 12	
Medium green	6	2½	96	2½ x 2½
Light green	3	4½	48	2½ x 4½
Light pink	2	2⅞	24	2⅞ x 2⅞
Blue	6	2½	96	2½ x 2½
Pieced border				
Medium green	1	4½	12	2½ x 4½
	1	2⅞	12	2⅞ x 2⅞
Light pink	1	2⅞	12	2⅞ x 2⅞
Blue	2	2½	28	2½ x 2½
	1	2⅞	8	2⅞ x 2⅞
	1	4½	8	2½ x 4½
Bright pink	3	2½	40	2½ x 2½
	1	2⅞	8	2⅞ x 2⅞
Binding				
Bright pink	7	2¼		

Press carefully after each step, following the direction of the pressing arrows.

Kansas Block

1. Refer to "Quick-Corner Triangles," page 106, and position a 2½" white square on a medium green 2½" x 4½" rectangle. Stitch to make a triangle corner. Press. Repeat to make a white triangle on the opposite end. Make four.

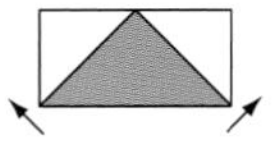

2. Sew 2½" bright pink squares on both sides of two of the units from step 1. Make two.

3. Sew the remaining units from step 1 to the top and bottom of the 4½" light green center square.

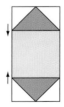

4. Sew the units from step 2 to the sides of the unit from step 3.

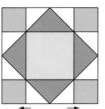

5. Repeat step 1 to sew two 2½" blue squares to a 2½" x 4½" white rectangle. Make four.

6. Referring to "Half-Square Triangles," page 105, position a 2⅞" bright pink square on a 2⅞" blue square. Stitch, cut, and press. Make four for a total of eight half-square triangle units.

7. Sew one unit from step 5 between two units from step 6. Press.

8. Sew two of the units from step 7 to the sides of the center unit from step 4.

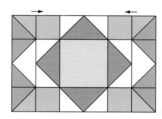

9. Sew 2½" blue squares to both ends of the remaining units from step 7 and sew to the top and bottom of the block.

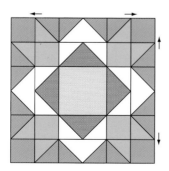

10. Repeat steps 1–9 to make a total of 13 Kansas blocks.

Windmill Block

1. Refer to "Quick Corner Triangle," page 106, and position a 2½" blue square on a 2½" x 4½" white rectangle. Stitch to make a triangle corner. Press. Repeat to make a blue triangle on the opposite end. Make four.

2. Sew a 2½" medium green square to each end of the units from step 1. Make four.

3. Repeat step 1 using white squares and a light green rectangle. Make four.

4. Sew a white rectangle to the unit from step 3 as shown. Make four.

5. Sew the four units from step 4 together as shown.

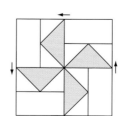

6. Sew two of the units from step 2 to the sides of the unit from step 5.

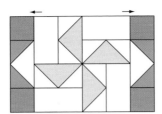

7. Refer to "Half-Square Triangles," page 105, and position a 2⅞" white square on a 2⅞" light pink square. Stitch, cut, and press. Make two to create four half-square triangle units.

8. Sew the units from step 7 to each end of the remaining units from step 2. Make two. Sew to the top and bottom to complete the block.

9. Repeat steps 1–8 to make a total of 12 Windmill blocks.

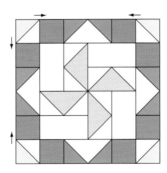

Assembly

Refer to the quilt layout on page 59. Beginning with a Kansas block and alternating with the Windmill blocks, lay out and sew the quilt in five rows with five blocks in each.

Pieced Border

1. Refer to "Quick Corner Triangles," page 106, and position a 2½" blue square on a 2½" x 4½" medium green rectangle. Stitch to make a triangle corner. Press. Repeat to make a blue triangle on the opposite end. Make twelve.

2. Sew bright pink squares to each end of the units from step 1. Make twelve.

3. Refer to "Half-Square Triangles," page 105, and position a 2⅞" light pink square on a 2⅞" medium green square and stitch. Cut and press. Make twelve to create twenty-four half-square triangle units.

4. Sew one of the units from step 3 to each end of the units from step 2 as shown. Make twelve.

5. As in step 3, position a 2⅞" bright pink square on a 2⅞" blue square and stitch. Cut and press. Make twelve to create twenty-four half-square triangle units.

6. Assemble two bright pink squares, one blue rectangle, and two of the units from step 5 as shown. Make eight.

7. Sew three units from step 4 alternately with two units from step 6 as shown in the quilt layout below. Make four border strips.

8. Sew two of the border units from step 7 to the sides of the quilt.

9. Add a blue square to each end of the two remaining border units and sew to the top and bottom of the quilt.

10. Referring to "Finishing the Quilt," page 108, layer and quilt as desired. Add binding to the quilt.

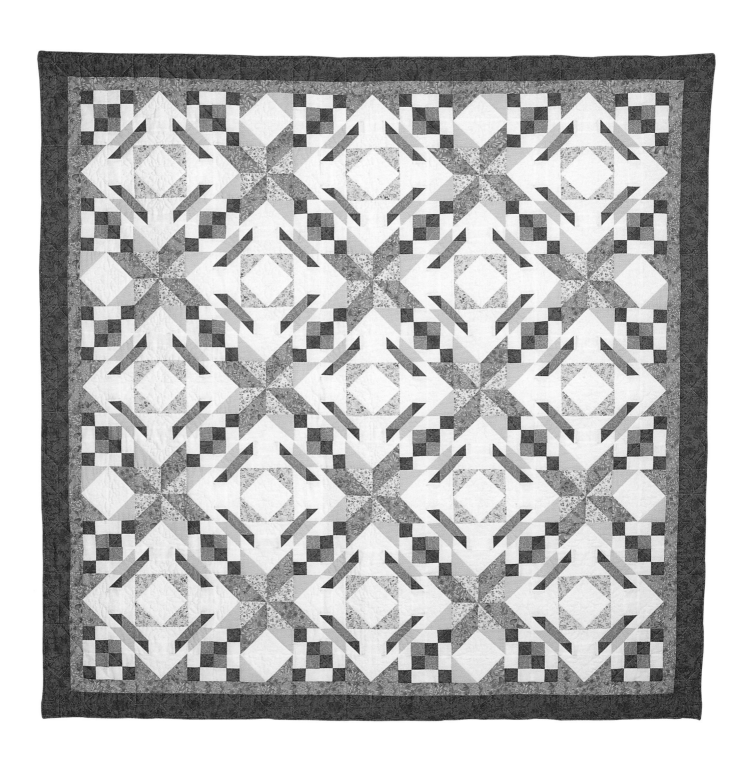

15 Two-Block Quilts

Pine Burr Star

Finished size: 75½" x 75½"

Blocks: Pine Burr and Pieced Star

The elements of these two blocks create a diagonal, on-point secondary design. The Pieced Star's colors are meant to be dominant to create the diagonal frames around the Pine Burr blocks.

Materials: 42"-wide fabric

White	3¾ yards
Yellow	1¼ yards
Bright blue (includes binding)	2¼ yards
Medium blue	⅞ yard
Yellow print	⅝ yard
Pink	1¾ yards
Pink print	½ yard
Backing	4½ yards
Batting	79" x 79"

Pieced Star

Pine Burr

Cut the following 42"-long strips and pieces.
Cutting sizes are given in inches.

CUTTING CHART

Fabric	Number of strips	Size	First Cut Number	First Cut Size
PINE BURR BLOCK		Finished size: 12"	Make 13	
White	10	2⅜	156	2⅜ x 2⅜
	3	6½	13	6½ x 6½
	5	3½	52	3½ x 3½
Yellow	7	2⅜	104	2⅜ x 2⅜
Bright blue	4	2⅜	52	2⅜ x 2⅜
Medium blue	7	2⅜	104	2⅜ x 2⅜
	3	2	52	2 x 2
Yellow print	5	3½	52	3½ x 3½
PIECED STAR BLOCK		Finished size 12"	Make 12	
White	5	2		
	5	6½	48	3½ x 6½
Yellow	5	3½	48	3½ x 3½
Bright blue	5	2		

Fabric	Number of strips	Size	First Cut Number	First Cut Size
PIECED STAR BLOCK (Continued)		Finished size 12"	Make 12	
Pink	5	3½	48	3½ x 3½
	3	3⅞	24	3⅞ x 3⅞
Pink print	3	3⅞	24	3⅞ x 3⅞
Pieced borders				
White	5	2		
	2	6½	20	3½ x 6½
Yellow	1	3½	8	3½ x 3½
Bright blue	4	2		
Medium blue	1	2		
Pink	3	3½	32	3½ x 3½
Outside borders and binding				
Pink (border)	8	2		
Bright blue (border)	8	3½		
(binding)	8	2¼		

Press carefully after each step, following the direction of the pressing arrows.

Pine Burr Block

1. Refer to "Half-Square Triangles," page 105, and position a 2⅜" white square on a 2⅜" yellow square. Stitch, cut, and press. Make four to create eight half-square triangle units.

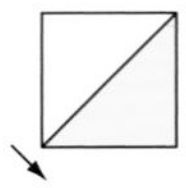

2. Repeat step 1 using four bright blue and four white squares to create eight half-square triangle units.

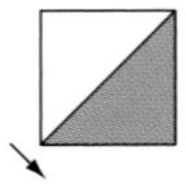

3. Repeat step 1 using four medium blue and four white squares to create eight half-square triangle units.

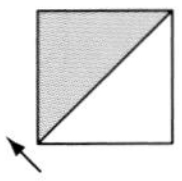

4. Repeat step 1 using two medium blue and two yellow squares to create four half-square triangle units.

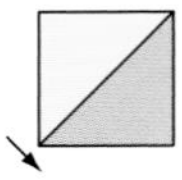

5. Refer to "Quick-Corner Triangles," page 106, and position a 3½" yellow print square in the corner of a 6½" white center square. Stitch to make the trian-

gle corner. Press. Repeat to make a triangle on all four corners.

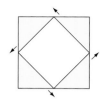

6. Sew the bright blue and white units from step 2 to the medium blue and white units from step 3 as shown. Make four of each.

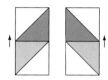

7. Sew the yellow and white units from step 1 to the medium blue and yellow units from step 4 as shown. Make two of each.

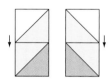

8. Sew yellow and white units to medium blue squares as shown. Make two of each.

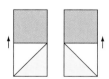

9. Sew two units from step 6 to a 3½" white square as shown. Make four.

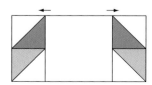

10. Sew the units from steps 7 and 8 together as shown. Make four.

11. Sew two of the units from step 9 to opposite sides of the unit from step 5 as shown.

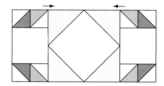

12. Sew the remaining units from step 9 to the units from 10 as shown.

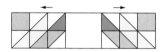

13. Sew the strips from step 12 to the center section from step 11 to complete the block.

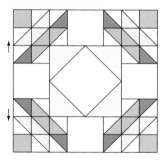

14. Repeat steps 1–13 to make a total of 13 Pine Burr blocks.

Pieced Star Block

1. Sew a 2"-wide bright blue strip and a 2"-wide white strip together lengthwise.

Cut crosswise into 2" segments. Cut eight.

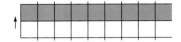

2. Sew units from step 1 into pairs. Make four.

3. Refer to "Quick-Corner Triangles," page 106, and position a 3½" yellow square on the left end of a 3½" x 6½" white rectangle. Stitch to make a triangle corner. Press. Repeat to make a pink triangle on the opposite end. Make four.

4. Refer to "Half-Square Triangles," page 105, and position a 3⅞" pink square on a 3⅞" pink print square. Stitch, cut, and press. Make two to create four half-square triangle units.

5. Sew the units from step 4 together as shown. Sew two units from step 3 to the sides.

 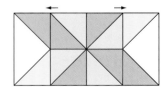

6. Sew the units from step 2 to both ends of the remaining two units from step 3. Sew to the top and bottom of the block.

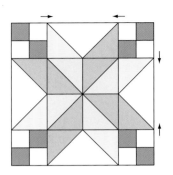

7. Repeat steps 1–6 to make a total of twelve Pieced Star blocks.

Assembly

Refer to the quilt layout on page 65. Beginning with a Pine Burr block and alternating with the Pieced Star blocks, lay out and sew the quilt in five rows with five blocks in each.

Pieced Border

1. Sew four 2"-wide bright blue strips and four 2"-wide white strips together lengthwise in pairs. Cut crosswise into 2" segments. Cut sixty-eight.

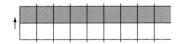

2. Sew a 2"-wide medium blue strip and a 2"-wide white strip together lengthwise. Cut crosswise into 2" segments. Cut twenty.

3. Sew forty-eight units from step 1 into pairs as shown to make twenty-four.

4. Sew the remaining units from step 1 to the units from step 2 as shown. Make twenty.

5. Repeat step 3 of the Pieced Star block to make eight units.

6. Repeat step 5 with both triangles pink. Make twelve units.

7. Sew the units from steps 3 and 6 as shown. Make twelve.

8. Sew the units from steps 4 and 5 as shown. Make eight.

9. Beginning with a unit from step 7, alternate three of the units from step 7 and two of the units from step 8 to create one pieced border strip as shown in the quilt layout below. Make four. Sew two of the border strips to the sides.

10. Sew the remaining four-patch blocks to both ends of the remaining pieced border strips. Sew to the top and bottom.

Finishing

1. Referring to "Adding the Borders" page 106, add the 2"-wide pink border and the 3½"-wide bright blue border to the quilt.

2. Referring to "Finishing the Quilt," page 108, layer and quilt as desired. Add binding to the quilt.

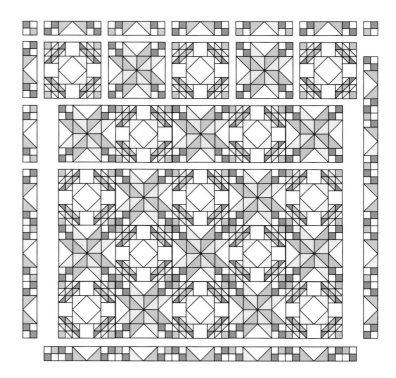

Road to Ohio by Way of Montana

Finished size: 68" x 92"

Blocks: Ohio Star and Road to Montana

The stepping-stone squares of the Road to Montana block give a connected look to the blocks. To vary the design, place outer stepping-stones in the corner of the Ohio Star Block, and another chain will form.

Materials: 42"-wide fabric

Assorted Reds	⅞ yard
Assorted Beiges	3½ yards
Assorted Greens	1⅜ yards
Green floral	2½ yards
Assorted Golds	½ yard
Brown (includes binding)	1⅛ yards
Peach	⅓ yard
Backing	5½ yards
Batting	72" x 96"

Road to Montana

Ohio Star

Cut the following 42"-long strips and pieces. Cutting sizes are given in inches.

CUTTING CHART

Fabric	Number of strips	Size	First Cut Number	First Cut Size
OHIO STAR BLOCK		Finished size: 12"	Make 18	
Red	5	2½		
Beige	5	2½		
	5	4½	72	2½ x 4½
	6	5¼	36	5¼ x 5¼
Green	6	5¼	36	5¼ x 5¼
Green floral	3	4½	18	4½ x 4½
ROAD TO MONTANA BLOCK		Finished size 12"	Make 17	
Red	5	2½		
Beige	19	2½	136	2½ x 2½

Fabric	Number of strips	Size	First Cut	
			Number	Size
ROAD TO MONTANA BLOCK (Continued)		Finished size 12"	Make 17	
Green floral	9	4½	68	4½ x 4½
Gold	5	2½		
Brown	3	4½	17	4½ x 4½
Outside borders and binding				
Green (border)	8	1½		
Green Floral (border)	9	3		
Peach (border)	8	1		
Brown (binding)	9	2¼		

Press carefully after each step, following the direction of the pressing arrows.

Ohio Star Block

1. Sew a 2½"-wide red strip and a 2½"-wide beige strip together lengthwise. Cut crosswise into 2½" segments. Cut four.

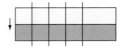

2. Sew one unit from step 1 to a 2½" x 4½" beige rectangle. Make four.

3. Refer to "Directional Triangles," page 105, and position a 5¼" beige square on a 5¼" green square. Stitch to the right of the drawn line, cut, and press. Make two to create eight directional triangles.

4. Sew the units from step 3 together as shown. Make four.

5. Sew two units from step 2 to one unit from step 4 as shown. Make two.

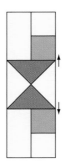

6. Sew the remaining two units from step 4 to the 4½" green floral square.

7. Sew the three sections together as shown to complete the block.

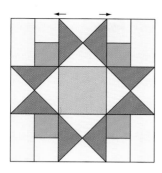

8. Repeat steps 1–7 to make a total of eighteen Ohio Star blocks.

Road to Montana Block

1. Sew a 2½"-wide red strip and a 2½"-wide beige strip together lengthwise. Cut crosswise into 2½" segments. Cut four.

2. Sew a 2½"-wide gold strip and a 2½"-wide beige strip together lengthwise. Cut crosswise into 2½" segments. Cut four.

3. Sew the units from steps 1 and 2 together as shown to make four.

4. Refer to "Quick-Corner Triangles," page 106, and position a 2½" beige square on the upper left corner of a 4½" green floral square. Stitch to make a triangle corner. Press and trim. Repeat to make a triangle on the upper right corner. Make four.

5. Sew two units from step 3 to one unit from step 4 as shown. Make two.

6. Sew two units from step 4 to the 4½" brown square as shown.

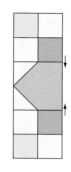

7. Sew the three sections together to complete the block.

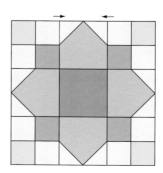

8. Repeat steps 1–7 to make a total of seventeen Road to Montana blocks.

Assembly

Refer to the quilt layout below. Beginning with an Ohio Star block and alternating with the Road to Montana blocks, lay out and sew the quilt in seven rows with five blocks in each.

Finishing

1. Referring to "Adding the Borders," page 106, add the 1½"-wide green border, the 1"-wide peach border, and the 3"-wide green floral border.

2. Referring to "Finishing the Quilt," page 108, layer and quilt as desired. Add binding to the quilt.

Dublin Square

Dublin Square

Finished size: 66" x 66"

Blocks: Dublin Steps and Town Square

When you combine these two blocks, a light, asymmetrical secondary star shows up. The large green triangles in Dublin Steps form a strong diagonal path across the quilt.

Materials: 42"-wide fabric

Beige	2⅛ yards
Green (includes binding)	2⅓ yards
Pink	1 yard
Gold	⅞ yard
Blue	⅔ yard
Backing	4⅛ yards
Batting	70" x 70"

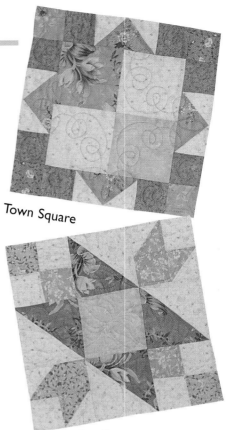

Town Square

Dublin Steps

Cut the following 42"-long strips and pieces.
Cutting sizes are given in inches.

CUTTING CHART

Fabric	Number of strips	Size	First Cut Number	First Cut Size
DUBLIN STEPS BLOCK		Finished size: 12"	Make 13	
Beige	4	4⅞	26	4⅞ x 4⅞
	2	2⅞	26	2⅞ x 2⅞
	6	2½	26	2½ x 2½
Green	4	4⅞	26	4⅞ x 4⅞
Pink	1	2⅞	13	2⅞ x 2⅞
	3	2½	13	2½ x 2½
	1	4½	5	4½ x 4½
Gold	1	2⅞	13	2⅞ x 2⅞
	1	4½	8	4½ x 4½
	3	2½	13	2½ x 2½
TOWN SQUARE BLOCK		Finished size 12"	Make 12	
Beige	4	4½		
	6	2½	96	2½ x 2½
Green	6	2½	96	2½ x 2½
Pink	2	4½		
	2	2½	24	2½ x 2½

Fabric	Number of strips	Size	First Cut	
			Number	Size
TOWN SQUARE BLOCK (Continued)		Finished size 12"	Make 12	
Gold	2	4½		
Blue	3	4½	48	2½ x 4½
	2	2½	24	2½ x 2½
Outside border and binding				
Green (border)	8	3½		
(binding)	7	2¼		

Press carefully after each step, following the direction of the pressing arrows.

Dublin Steps Block

1. Refer to "Half-Square Triangles," page 105, and position a 4⅞" beige square on a 4⅞" green square. Stitch, cut, and press. Make two to create four half-square triangle units.

2. Repeat step 1 using a 2⅞" beige square and a 2⅞" pink square. Make one to create two half-square triangle units.

3. Repeat step 1 using a 2⅞" beige square and a 2⅞" gold square. Make one to create two half-square triangle units.

4. Sew a 2½"-wide pink strip and a 2½"-wide beige strip together lengthwise. Cut crosswise into 2½" segments. Cut two.

5. Sew a 2½"-wide gold strip and a 2½"-wide beige strip together lengthwise. Cut crosswise into 2½" segments. Cut two.

6. Sew the corner squares using segments from steps 4 and 5 as shown. Make two.

7. Using the units from step 2, a 2½" beige square, and a 2½" pink square, make one corner square as shown.

8. Using the units from step 3, a beige square, and a gold square, make one corner square as shown.

9. Sew the left section of the block as shown, using one unit from step 1, one unit from step 6, and the unit from step 8.

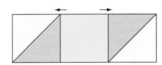

10. Sew the center section of the block as shown, using two units from step 1 and the gold center square.

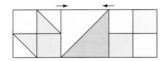

11. Sew the right section of the block as shown, using one unit from step 1, one unit from step 6, and the unit from step 7.

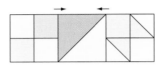

12. Sew the units from steps 9, 10, and 11 to complete the outer Dublin Steps block with a gold center. Make eight.

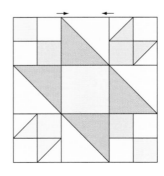

13. Repeat steps 1–12 except use pink squares in step 10 to make a total of five Dublin Steps blocks with pink centers.

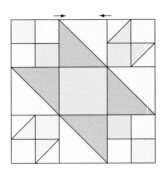

Town Square Block

1. Sew a 4½"-wide pink strip and a 4½"-wide beige strip together lengthwise. Sew a 4½"-wide gold strip and 4½" beige strip together lengthwise. Cut one 4½"-wide segment crosswise from each strip.

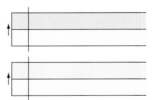

2. Sew the segments from each pieced strip together as shown.

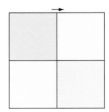

3. Refer to "Quick-Corner Triangles," page 106, and position a 2½" beige square on a 2½" x 4½" blue rectangle. Stitch to make a triangle corner. Press and

trim. Repeat to make a triangle on the other corner. Make a total of four.

4. Sew one 2½" green square to each end of the unit from step 3. Make four.

5. Sew one unit from step 4 to each side of the unit from step 2.

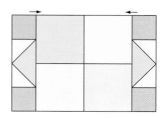

6. Sew a 2½" blue square to the right end, and a 2½" pink square to the left end of a unit from step 5. Make two.

7. Sew the units from step 6 to the top and bottom of the unit from step 5 to complete the block.

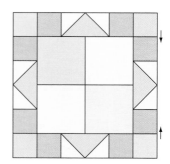

8. Repeat steps 1–7 to make a total of twelve Town Square blocks.

Assembly

Refer to the quilt layout below. Beginning with a Dublin Steps block and alternating with the Town Square blocks, lay out the quilt in five rows with five blocks in each. Arrange the Dublin Steps blocks with pink centers in the interior of the quilt top and the Dublin Steps blocks with gold centers around the outside.

Finishing

1. Referring to "Adding the Borders," page 106, add 3½"-wide green border strips to the quilt.

2. Referring to "Finishing the Quilt," page 108, layer, baste, and quilt as desired. Add binding to the quilt.

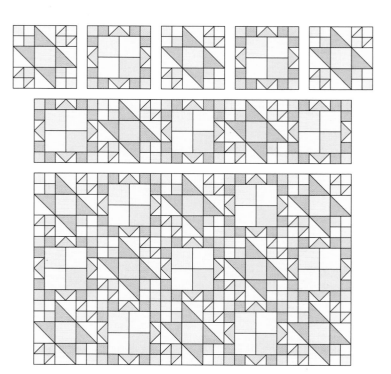

Churn Dash Memories

Finished size: 68" x 68"

Blocks: Memories and Churn Dash variation

The turquoise triangles of each block connect to form a broken, on-point square. The empty aqua spaces help the eye to connect the lines between the two blocks, making them appear unbroken.

Materials: 42"-wide fabric

Aqua	3 yards
Dark print	1⅛ yards
Turquoise	1⅝ yards
Blue (includes binding)	1⅝ yards
Yellow	⅝ yard
Lavender	¾ yard
Blue/lavender	⅝ yard
Backing	4⅛ yards
Batting	72" x 72"

Memories

Churn Dash variation

Cut the following 42"-long strips and pieces. Cutting sizes are given in inches.

CUTTING CHART

Fabric	Number of strips	Size	First Cut Number	First Cut Size	Second Cut
MEMORIES BLOCK			Finished size: 12"		Make 13
Aqua	4	2⅞	52	2⅞ x 2⅞	
	4	2½	52	2½ x 2½	
	4	4½	52	2½ x 4½	
Dark print	4	2⅞	52	2⅞ x 2⅞	
	2	4½	13	4½ x 4½	
Turquoise	7	2½	104	2½ x 2½	
	4	4½	52	2½ x 4½	
Blue	7	2½	104	2½ x 2½	
Yellow	4	2½	52	2½ x 2½	
CHURN DASH VARIATION BLOCK			Finished size 12"		Make 12
Aqua	3	4⅞	24	4⅞ x 4⅞	diagonally once
	6	2½			
Dark print	2	2⅞	24	2⅞ x 2⅞	
Turquoise	4	2⅞	48	2⅞ x 2⅞	diagonally once

Fabric	Number of strips	Size	First Cut Number	First Cut Size	Second Cut
CHURN DASH VARIATION BLOCK (Continued)			Finished size 12"		Make 12
Blue	2	2⅞	24	2⅞ x 2⅞	
Yellow	2	2⅞	24	2⅞ x 2⅞	
Lavender	2	2⅞	24	2⅞ x 2⅞	
Blue/lavender	6	2½			
Pieced border					
Aqua	2	4⅞	12	4⅞ x 4⅞	diagonally once
	2	4½	20	2½ x 4½	
	1	2½	16	2½ x 2½	
	1	5¼	4	5¼ x 5¼	
	1	2⅞	4	2⅞ x 2⅞	diagonally once
Dark print	2	4⅞	10	4⅞ x 4⅞	diagonally once
Turquoise	2	2⅞	24	2⅞ x 2⅞	diagonally once
	1	2½	16	2½ x 2½	
	1	4½	8	2½ x 4½	
Blue	1	2⅞	12	2⅞ x 2⅞	
	2	2½	24	2½ x 2½	
Lavender	1	2⅞	12	2⅞ x 2⅞	
	1	4½	12	2½ x 4½	
	1	5¼	4	5¼ x 5¼	
	1	2½	4	2½ x 2½	
BINDING					
Blue	8	2¼			

Press carefully after each step, following the direction of the pressing arrows.

Memories Block

1. Refer to "Half-Square Triangles," page 105, and position a 2⅞" aqua square on a 2⅞" dark print square. Stitch, cut, and press. Make four to create eight half-square triangle units.

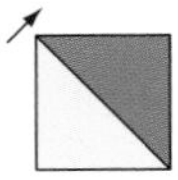

2. Refer to "Quick-Corner Triangles," page 106, and position a 2½" turquoise square on a 2½" x 4½" aqua rectangle. Stitch to make a triangle corner. Press and trim. Repeat to make a triangle on the opposite corner. Make four.

3. Repeat step 2 using 2½" blue squares on a 2½" x 4½" turquoise rectangle. Make four.

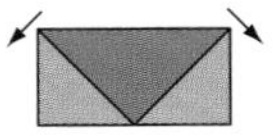

4. Sew units from step 2 to the units from step 3 as shown. Make four.

5. Using two of the triangle units from step 1, one 2½" yellow square, and one 2½" aqua square, sew the block corners as shown. Make four.

6. Sew one unit from step 4 between two corner units from step 5. Make two.

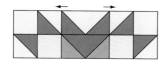

7. Sew the remaining two units from step 4 to the 4½" dark print center square.

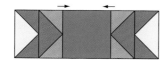

8. Sew together the top, middle, and bottom sections as shown.

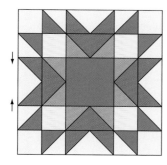

9. Repeat steps 1–8 to make a total of 13 Memories blocks.

Churn Dash Variation Block

1. Refer to "Half-Square Triangles," page 105, and position a 2⅞" yellow square on a 2⅞" dark print square. Stitch, cut, and press. Make two to create four half-square triangle units.

2. Sew together all four units from step 1 as shown.

3. Repeat step 1 using a 2⅞" blue square and a 2⅞" lavender square. Make two to create four half-square triangle units.

4. Sew two turquoise triangles to the units from step 3 as shown. Make four.

5. Sew the large aqua triangles to the units from step 4 as shown. Make four.

6. Sew a 2½" x 42" blue/lavender strip and a 2½" x 42" aqua strip together lengthwise. Cut crosswise into 4½" segments. Cut four.

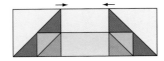

7. Sew a unit from step 6 between two corner units from step 5 to make the top and bottom block sections. Make two.

8. Sew the center triangle unit from step 2 between the two remaining units from step 6.

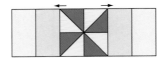

9. Sew together the top, bottom, and middle sections as shown to complete the block.

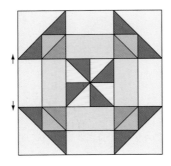

10. Repeat steps 1–9 to make a total of twelve Churn Dash variation blocks.

Assembly

Refer to the quilt layout on page 82. Beginning with a Memories block and alternating with the Churn Dash variation blocks, lay out and sew the quilt in five rows with five blocks in each.

Pieced Border

1. Repeat steps 3, 4, and 5 from the Churn Dash variation block. Make twenty-four.

2. Refer to "Quick-Corner Triangles," page 106, and position a 2½" blue square on a 2½" x 4½" lavender rectangle. Stitch to make a triangle corner. Press and trim. Repeat to make a triangle on the opposite end. Make twelve.

3. Sew the triangle units from step 2 to the 2½" x 4½" aqua rectangles. Make twelve.

4. Sew one unit from step 3 between two units from step 1. Make twelve.

5. Repeat step 2, positioning turquoise squares on the aqua rectangles. Stitch to make triangle corners. Trim and press. Make eight.

6. Repeat step 5, reversing the colors. Make eight.

7. Stitch the units from step 5 to the units from step 6 as shown. Make eight.

8. Refer to "Half-Square Triangles," page 105, and position a 5¼" lavender square on a 5¼" aqua square and stitch. Cut and press. Cut in half diagonally as shown. Make four to create sixteen units.

9. Sew a dark print triangle to the units from step 8 as shown. Make eight of each.

10. Stitch one unit from step 7 between two units from step 9. Make eight.

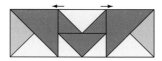

11. To make the corner border squares, sew two aqua triangles to a lavender square as shown. Make four.

12. Sew a dark print triangle to each of the units from step 11 to complete the four corner squares.

13. Beginning with a step 4 unit and alternating with the step 10 units, lay out and sew the border strips in four rows with five units in each as shown in the quilt layout on page 82.

14. Sew two of the border strips from step 13 to the sides of the quilt.

15. Sew the corner squares from step 12 to each end of the remaining border strips and sew them to the top and bottom.

16. Referring to "Finishing the Quilt," page 108, layer, baste, and quilt as desired. Add binding to the quilt.

15 Two-Block Quilts

Swallow's Star Path

Swallow's Star Path

Finished size: 103" x 103"

Blocks: Swallow in the Window variation and Diamond Path

The blue stepping-stone squares in the Diamond Path blocks create a diagonal connection between the blocks. The stepping-stone pattern is mirrored in the centers of the swallow blocks.

Materials: 42"-wide fabric

Light yellow	$7/8$ yard
Dark blue (includes binding)	$4 5/8$ yards
Floral	$3 1/4$ yards
Medium blue	$1 3/4$ yards
White	$3 3/4$ yards
Bright yellow	$2 1/3$ yards
Backing	9 yards
Batting	107" x 107"

Swallow in the Window variation

Diamond Path

Cut the following 42"-long strips and pieces. Cutting sizes are given in inches.

CUTTING CHART

Fabric	Number of strips	Size	First Cut Number	First Cut Size	Second Cut
SWALLOW IN THE WINDOW VARIATION BLOCK			Finished size: 16"	Make 13	
Light yellow	9	$2 1/2$	104	$2 1/2 \times 2 1/2$	
Dark blue	9	$2 1/2$	104	$2 1/2 \times 2 1/2$	
	4	$2 7/8$	52	$2 7/8 \times 2 7/8$	
Floral	4	$4 1/2$	52	$2 1/2 \times 4 1/2$	
	4	$9 1/4$	13	$9 1/4 \times 9 1/4$	diagonally twice
Medium blue	10	$2 1/2$	156	$2 1/2 \times 2 1/2$	
	4	$2 7/8$	52	$2 7/8 \times 2 7/8$	
White	7	$4 1/2$	104	$2 1/2 \times 4 1/2$	
	4	$2 7/8$	52	$2 7/8 \times 2 7/8$	diagonally once
	4	$2 1/2$	52	$2 1/2 \times 2 1/2$	
DIAMOND PATH BLOCK			Finished size 16"	Make 12	
Dark blue	8	$2 1/2$			
Medium blue	3	$2 1/2$	48	$2 1/2 \times 2 1/2$	

CUTTING CHART (continued)

Fabric	Number of strips	Size	First Cut Number	First Cut Size	Second Cut
DIAMOND PATH BLOCK (Continued)			Finished size 16"		Make 12
White	6	4½	48	4½ x 4½	
	6	4⅞	48	4⅞ x 4⅞	diagonally once
Bright yellow	14	2½	96	2½ x 2½	
	4	2⅞	48	2⅞ x 2⅞	diagonally once
	2	5¼	6	5¼ x 5¼	diagonally twice
Pieced Border					
Dark blue	6	2½	56	2½ x 2½	
	2	2⅞	16	2⅞ x 2⅞	
Floral	2	4⅞	12	4⅞ x 4⅞	
	5	4½	72	2½ x 4½	
	2	2⅞	16	2⅞ x 2⅞	
	4	2½	48	2½ x 2½, then cut four 2½ x 6½	
	1	4½	8	4½ x 4½	
Medium blue	2	2⅞	16	2⅞ x 2⅞	
	2	2½	32	2½ x 2½	
White	2	4⅞	12	4⅞ x 4⅞	
	1	4½	8	2½ x 4½	
Bright yellow	3	2½	16	2½ x 2½	
Outside borders and binding					
Dark blue (border)	12	5			
(binding)	11	2¼			
Bright yellow (border)	9	1½			

Press carefully after each step, following the direction of the pressing arrows or open as indicated.

Swallow in the Window Variation Block

1. Sew a 2½"-wide light yellow strip and a 2½"-wide dark blue strip together lengthwise. Crosscut into 2½" segments. Cut two.

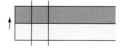

2. Sew the two units from step 1 together as shown.

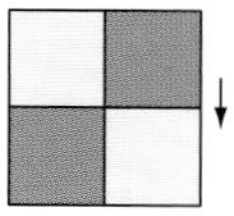

3. Refer to "Quick-Corner Triangles," page 106, and position a 2½" light yellow square on a 2½" x 4½" floral rectangle. Stitch to make a triangle corner. Press and trim. Repeat to make a triangle on the opposite corner. Make a total of four.

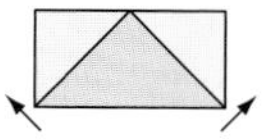

4. Attach a unit from step 3 to each side of the unit from step 2.

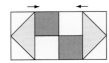

5. Sew a medium blue 2½" square to each end of the two remaining units from step 3.

6. Sew the units from step 5 to the sides of the unit from step 4.

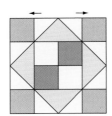

7. Refer to "Half-Square Triangles," page 105, and position a 2⅞" medium blue square on a 2⅞" dark blue square. Stitch, cut, and press. Make two to create four half-square triangle units. Press open.

8. Repeat step 3, using a 2½" dark blue square on the left and a 2½" medium blue square on the right of a 2½" x 4½" white rectangle. Stitch, trim, and press. Make eight.

9. Sew a white triangle on the left side of a unit from step 8 and a white square on the right, as shown. Make four.

10. Sew a white triangle on the right side of the remaining four units from step 8.

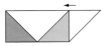

11. Sew a dark blue triangle to the left side and a medium blue triangle to the bottom of a unit from step 7. Make four.

12. Using a unit each from steps 9, 10, and 11, sew a block corner unit. Repeat to make a total of four.

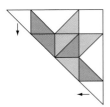

13. Sew the large floral triangles to all four sides of the unit from step 6.

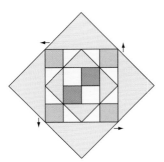

14. Sew the corner units from step 12 to each side of the unit from step 13 to complete the block.

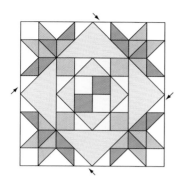

15. Repeat steps 1–14 to make a total of thirteen Swallow in the Window variation blocks.

Diamond Path Block

1. Repeat steps 1 and 2 from the Swallow in the Window variation block, using dark blue and bright yellow 2½" strips. Crosscut into ten 2½" segments. Make five.

2. Sew a bright yellow triangle to the top and right sides of a medium blue 2½" square. Make four.

3. Refer to "Quick-Corner Triangles," page 106, and position a 2½" bright yellow square on the upper left corner of a 4½" x 4½" white square. Stitch to

make a triangle corner. Press and trim. Repeat to make a triangle on the upper right corner. Make a total of four.

4. Sew a unit from step 2 to both sides of a unit from step 3. Make two.

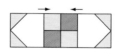

5. Sew a unit from step 3 to either side of a unit from step 1.

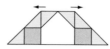

6. Sew the units from steps 4 and 5 together as shown.

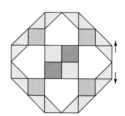

7. Add the bright yellow triangles to the top and bottom of the unit from step 6.

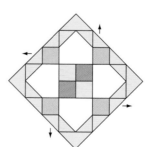

8. Sew a large white triangle to two sides of a unit from step 1. Repeat to make a total of four.

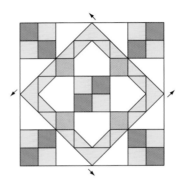

9. Attach the four units from step 8 to sides of the unit from step 7 to complete the block.

10. Repeat steps 1–9 to make a total of twelve Diamond Path blocks.

Assembly

Refer to the quilt layout on page 90. Beginning with a Swallow in the Window Variation block and alternating with the Diamond Path blocks, lay out and sew the quilt in five rows with five blocks in each.

Pieced Border

1. Repeat steps 1 and 2 from the Swallow in the Window variation block using dark blue and bright yellow 2½" strips. Make twenty-eight.

2. Refer to "Half-Square Triangles," page 105, and position a 4⅞" white square on a 4⅞" floral square. Stitch, cut, and press. Make twelve to create twenty-four half-square triangle units.

3. Sew three 2½" x 4½" floral rectangles and two 2½" dark blue squares as shown. Make twelve.

4. Using two units each from steps 1 and 2 and one unit from step 3, sew as shown. Make twelve.

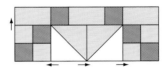

5. Repeat step 2, positioning a 2⅞" medium blue square on a 2⅞" dark blue square. Stitch, cut, and press. Make eight to create sixteen half-square triangle units. Press open.

6. Repeat step 2 and position a 2⅞" floral square on a 2⅞" dark blue square. Stitch, cut, and press. Make eight to create sixteen half-square triangle units.

7. Repeat step 2 and position a 2⅞" medium blue square on a 2⅞" floral square. Stitch, cut, and press. Make eight to create sixteen half-square triangle units.

8. Refer to "Quick-Corner Triangles," page 106, and position a 2½" dark blue square on the left corner of a 2½" x 4½" floral rectangle. Stitch to make a triangle corner. Press and trim. Repeat to make a medium blue triangle on the opposite corner. Make a total of thirty-two.

9. Repeat step 8 and position a 2½" floral square on the 2½" x 4½" white rectangle. Stitch to make a triangle corner. Press and trim. Repeat to make a triangle on the opposite end. Make a total of eight.

10. Repeat step 3 of the Diamond Path block, positioning a 2½" bright yellow square on the corners of a 4½" x 4½" floral square. Stitch to make triangle corners. Press and trim. Make a total of eight.

11. Using a unit each from steps 5, 6, and 7 and a 2½" floral square, sew sixteen as shown.

12. Sew two units from step 8, a unit from step 11, and a 2½" floral square together as shown. Make sixteen.

13. Sew two units from step 12, one unit from step 10, and one unit from step 9 as shown. Make eight.

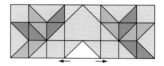

14. Sew a 2½" x 4½" floral rectangle to one side of the remaining four units from step 1. Make four.

15. Sew a 2½" x 6½" floral rectangle to the units from step 14. Make four border corners.

16. Sew three units from step 4 and two units from step 13 together to make a side border as shown in the quilt layout below. Make four.

17. Sew two of the borders to the sides of the quilt.

18. Add a border corner to each end of the two remaining borders. Sew to the top and bottom of the quilt.

Finishing

1. Referring to "Adding the Borders," page 106, add the 1½"-wide bright yellow border and the 5"-wide dark blue border to the quilt.

2. Referring to "Finishing the Quilt," page 108, layer, baste, and quilt as desired. Add binding to the quilt.

Tippecanoe Mosaic

Tippecanoe Mosaic

Finished size: 72" x 72"

Blocks: Mosaic and Tippecanoe

Using bright, vibrant colors in the Mosaic blocks will bring them to the forefront, and soft colors in the Tippecanoe blocks will cause them to recede into the background.

Materials: 42"-wide fabric

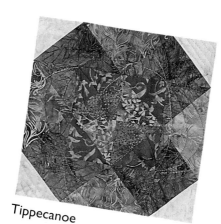

Tippecanoe

Beige	¾ yard
Purple	2½ yards
Bright pink	⅝ yard
Dark green (includes binding)	2 yards
Pink/green	2⅜ yards
Green/yellow	⅓ yard
Purple/green	½ yard
Lavender	⅓ yard
Medium green	1⅓ yards
Backing	4¼ yards
Batting	76" x 76"

Mosaic

Cut the following 42"-long strips and pieces.
Cutting sizes are given in inches.

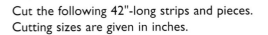

CUTTING CHART

Fabric	Number of strips	Size	First Cut Number	First Cut Size
MOSAIC BLOCK		Finished size: 12"	Make 13	
Beige	3	3⅞	24	3⅞ x 3⅞
Purple	3	3⅞	26	3⅞ x 3⅞
	5	3½	52	3½ x 3½
Bright pink	3	3⅞	28	3⅞ x 3⅞
Dark green	3	3⅞	26	3⅞ x 3⅞
	5	3½	52	3½ x 3½
Pink/green	5	6½	52	3½ x 6½
TIPPECANOE BLOCK		Finished size 12"	Make 12	
Beige	3	3⅞	24	3⅞ x 3⅞
Pink/green	5	6½	48	3½ x 6½
Green/yellow	2	3⅞	12	3⅞ x 3⅞

Fabric	Number of strips	Size	First Cut	
			Number	Size
TIPPECANOE BLOCK		Finished size 12"	Make 12	
Purple/green	3	3⅞	24	3⅞ x 3⅞
Lavender	2	3⅞	12	3⅞ x 3⅞
Medium green	9	3½	96	3½ x 3½
	3	3⅞	24	3⅞ x 3⅞
Pieced border				
Purple	7	3½	72	3½ x 3½
	1	3⅞	6	3⅞ x 3⅞
Bright pink	1	3⅞	6	3⅞ x 3⅞
Dark green	2	6½	16	3½ x 6½
Pink/green	2	6½	20	3½ x 6½
Outside border and binding				
Purple (border)	8	3½		
Dark green (binding)	8	2¼		

Press carefully after each step, referring to the arrows in each illustration for pressing directions.

Mosaic Block

1. Refer to "Half-Square Triangles," page 105, and position a 3⅞" beige square on a purple 3⅞" square. Stitch, cut and press. Make two to create four half-square triangle units.

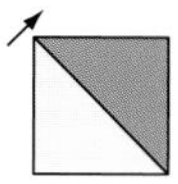

2. Repeat step 1 using 3⅞" bright pink and dark green squares. Make two to create four half-square triangle units.

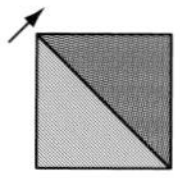

3. Refer to "Quick-Corner Triangles," page 106, and position a 3½" purple square on the upper left of a 3½" x 6½" pink/green rectangle. Stitch to make a triangle corner. Press. Repeat to make a dark green triangle on the opposite end. Make four.

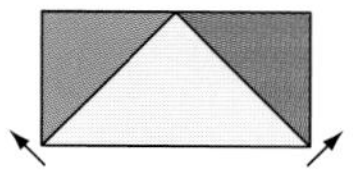

4. Sew together all four of the units from step 2 as shown.

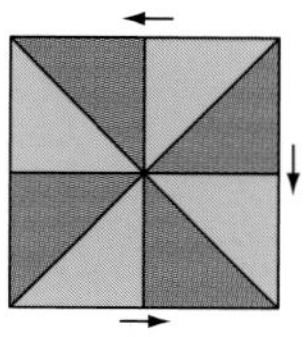

5. Stitch a unit from step 3 to opposite sides of the unit from step 4.

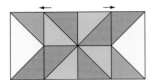

6. Stitch the units from step 1 to each end of the remaining units from step 3. Make two. Sew to the top and bottom to complete the block.

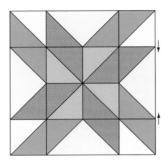

7. Repeat steps 1–6 to make a total of nine Mosaic blocks.

8. To make the corner Mosaic blocks, repeat steps 1–6, but in step 1 use three purple/beige half-square triangle units and one purple/bright pink half-square triangle units as shown. Make four.

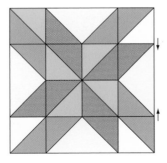

Tippecanoe Block

1. Repeat step 1 of the Mosaic block and position a 3⅞" green/yellow square on a 3⅞" purple/green square and stitch. Cut and press. Make one to create two half-square triangle units.

2. Repeat step 1 using a lavender and a purple/green square. Stitch the units from steps 1 and 2 together as shown.

3. Repeat step 3 of the Mosaic block and position a 3½" medium green square on the left end of a pink/green rectangle. Stitch to make a triangle corner. Press. Repeat to make a medium green triangle on the opposite end. Make four.

4. Repeat step 1, using a 3⅞" medium green square and a 3⅞" beige square. Make two to create four half-square triangle units.

5. Sew two of the units from step 3 to the sides of the unit from step 2.

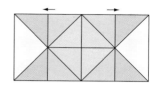

6. Sew a unit from step 4 to each end of the two remaining units from step 3. Sew to the top and bottom to complete the block.

7. Repeat steps 1–7 to make a total of 12 Tippecanoe blocks.

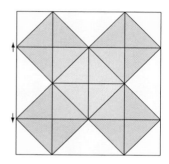

Assembly

Refer to the quilt layout on page 96. Beginning with a Mosaic block and alternating with the Tippecanoe blocks, lay out and sew the quilt in five rows with five blocks in each, being careful to correctly place the four corner Mosaic blocks in the correct position.

Pieced Border

1. Refer to "Quick-Corner Triangles," page 106, and position a 3 1/2" purple square on a 3 1/2" x 6 1/2" pink/green rectangle. Stitch to make a triangle corner. Press. Repeat to make a purple triangle on the opposite end. Make twenty.

2. Repeat step 1, positioning a 3 1/2" purple square on a 3 1/2" x 6 1/2" dark green rectangle. Stitch to make a triangle corner. Press. Repeat to make a purple triangle on the opposite end. Make sixteen.

3. Using five of the units from step 1 and four of the units from step 2, assemble the borders as shown on page 96. Make four.

4. Repeat step 1, positioning a 3 7/8" bright pink square on a 3 7/8" purple square and stitch. Cut and press. Make six to create twelve half-square triangle units.

5. Sew a corner square to each end of the border strips. Attach the side borders.

6. Add a corner square from step 4 to each end of the remaining two border strips. Sew to the top and bottom of the quilt.

Finishing

1. Referring to "Adding the Borders," page 106, add the 3½"-wide purple borders to the quilt.

2. Referring to "Finishing the Quilt," page 108, layer, baste, and quilt as desired. Add binding to the quilt.

Wild Asters

Wild Asters

Finished size: 62" x 62"

Blocks: Double Aster and Wild Goose Chase

The Double Aster blocks in this quilt are dominant so choose bolder colors for them. The Wild Goose Chase blocks will appear to fade into the background by using softer, subtler colors.

Materials: 42"-wide fabric

White	1 1/3 yards
Navy (includes binding)	2 7/8 yards
Teal	3/4 yard
Purple	1 1/2 yards
Light teal	1/3 yard
Gray	7/8 yard
Blue	5/8 yard
Backing	3 3/4 yards
Batting	66" x 66"

Wild Goose Chase

Double Aster

Cut the following 42"-long strips and pieces. Cutting sizes are given in inches.

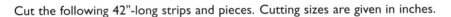

CUTTING CHART

Fabric	Number of strips	Size	First Cut Number	First Cut Size	Second Cut
DOUBLE ASTER BLOCK			Finished size: 10"		Make 13
White	4	2 7/8	52	2 7/8 x 2 7/8	26 diagonally once
	4	2 1/2	52	2 1/2 x 2 1/2	
	2	3 1/4	13	3 1/4 x 3 1/4	
Navy	2	2 7/8	26	2 7/8 x 2 7/8	
	2	3 1/4	13	3 1/4 x 3 1/4	
Teal	2	5 1/4	13	5 1/4 x 5 1/4	diagonally twice
	1	2 1/2	13	2 1/2 x 2 1/2	
Purple	4	4 7/8	26	4 7/8 x 4 7/8	diagonally once
WILD GOOSE CHASE BLOCK			Finished size 10"		Make 12
Purple	2	2 7/8	24	2 7/8 x 2 7/8	
	1	2 1/2	12	2 1/2 x 2 1/2	
Light teal	2	2 7/8	24	2 7/8 x 2 7/8	
Gray	4	2 7/8	48	2 7/8 x 2 7/8	diagonally once
	3	4 1/2	48	2 1/2 x 4 1/2	
Blue	3	4 7/8	24	4 7/8 x 4 7/8	diagonally once

Fabric	Number of strips	Size	First Cut Number	First Cut Size	Second Cut
Pieced borders					
White	2	2⅞	20	2⅞ x 2⅞	
	4	2½	20	2½ x 2½	
Navy	5	2⅞	54	2⅞ x 2⅞	
Teal	3	2⅞	36	2⅞ x 2⅞	
Purple	4	2⅞	42	2⅞ x 2⅞	
	3	2½	4	2½ x 2½	
Outside border and binding					
Navy (border)	8	2½			
(binding)	7	2¼			

Press carefully after each step, following the direction of the pressing arrows.

Double Aster Block

1. Refer to "Half-Square Triangles," page 105, and position a 2⅞" white square on a 2⅞" navy square. Stitch, cut, and press. Make two to create four half-square triangle units.

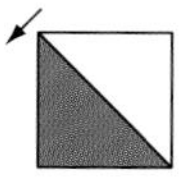

2. Sew a unit from step 1 to a 2½" white square. Make four.

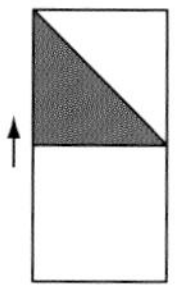

3. Refer to "Directional Triangles," page 105, and position a 3¼" white square on a 3¼" navy square. Stitch to the left of the drawn line, cut, and press. Make one to create four quarter-square triangle units.

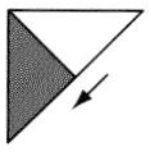

4. Sew a white triangle to a unit from step 3 as shown. Make four.

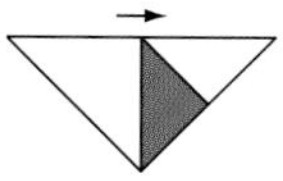

5. Sew a teal triangle to the unit from step 4. Make four.

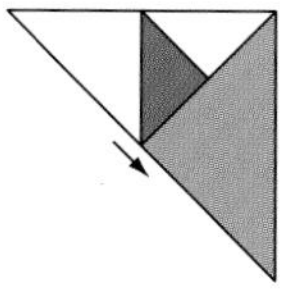

6. Sew a purple triangle to the unit from step 5. Make four.

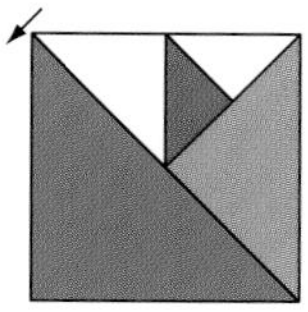

7. Sew the unit from step 2 to the unit from step 6 as shown. Make four.

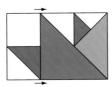

8. Using a partial seam as shown, sew the teal center square to one end of a unit from step 7.

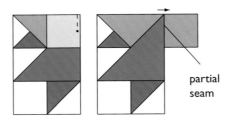

partial seam

9. Sew the next step 7 unit to the top as shown.

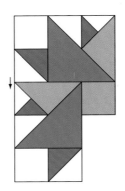

10. Sew the third step 7 unit to the right side as shown.

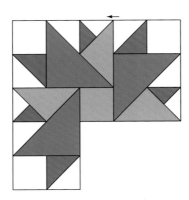

11. Sew the final step 7 unit to the bottom and complete the partial seam from step 8.

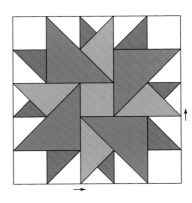

12. Repeat steps 1–11 to make a total of thirteen Double Aster blocks.

Wild Goose Chase Block

1. Repeat step 1 of the Double Aster block by positioning a 2⅞" light teal square on a 2⅞" purple square. Stitch, cut, and press. Make two to create four half-square triangle units.

2. Sew a gray triangle to two sides of the unit from step 1. Make four.

3. Sew a blue triangle to the unit from step 2. Make four.

4. Sew a 2½" x 4½" gray rectangle between two units from step 3. Make two.

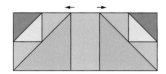

5. Sew two 2½" x 4½" gray rectangles to one 2½" x 2½" purple square.

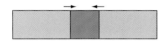

6. Sew the unit from step 5 between two units from step 4 to complete the block.

7. Repeat steps 1–6 to make a total of twelve Wild Goose Chase blocks.

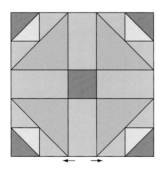

Assembly

Refer to the quilt layout on page 103. Beginning with a Double Aster block and alternating with the Wild Goose Chase blocks, lay out and sew the quilt in five rows with five blocks in each.

Pieced Border

1. Repeat step 1 of the Double Aster block by positioning a 2⅞" white square on a 2⅞" navy square. Stitch, cut, and press. Make twenty to create forty half-square triangle units.

2. Repeat step 1 by positioning a 2⅞" teal square on a 2⅞" navy square. Stitch, cut, and press. Make fourteen to create twenty-eight half-square triangle units.

3. Repeat step 1 by positioning a 2⅞" purple square on a 2⅞" navy square. Stitch, cut, and press. Make twenty to create forty half-square triangle units.

4. Repeat step 1 by positioning a 2⅞" teal square on a 2⅞" purple square. Stitch, cut, and press. Make twenty-two to create forty-four half-square triangle units.

5. Combine one unit each from steps 1–4 as shown. Make twelve of each.

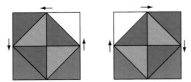

6. Using a 2½" white square and one unit each from steps 1, 3 and 4, make eight of each as shown.

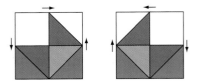

7. Sew a 2½" purple strip and a 2½" white strip together lengthwise. Cut crosswise into 2½" segments. Cut twenty.

8. Sew two units from step 5 to one unit from step 7 as shown. Make twelve.

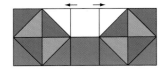

9. Sew two units from step 6 to one unit from step 7 as shown. Make eight.

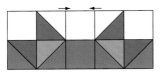

10. Using a 2½" white square, a 2½" purple square, and a unit from steps 2 and 4, sew the corner squares as shown. Make four.

11. Beginning with a unit from step 8 and alternating with the units from step 9, sew the borders in four rows with five border sections in each.

12. Sew a border strip to each side of the quilt top.

13. Sew a corner square from step 10 to each end of the two remaining border strips and sew them to the top and bottom.

Finishing

1. Referring to " Adding the Borders," page 106, add the 2½"-wide navy border strips to the quilt.

2. Referring to "Finishing the Quilt," page 108, layer, baste, and quilt as desired. Add binding to the quilt.

General Directions

When you go shopping to find just the right combination of fabrics for your two-block quilt, be sure to select fabric that is 100% cotton. Usually they will be about 42"-wide, and the fabric requirements in this book are based on that width. Once you get your fabrics home, pre-wash, dry, and press them before cutting to eliminate any chance of shrinking.

Before starting a new project, putting a new blade in your rotary cutter will save you time later. A sharp blade will make it easier to cut accurate pieces, and accurate pieces will help your blocks fit together easily.

The next thing to check is the seam allowance guide on your sewing machine. Seams should be sewn with a scant ¼" seam allowance. Making accurate seams is another way to ensure that your blocks come out perfectly. To find the "perfect ¼" seam" on your machine, cut three 1½" strips about 6"–8" in length, and sew the long edges of the strips together, pressing the seams towards the outside strips.

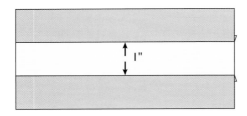

The center strip should measure exactly 1" in width if your seams are the correct scant ¼" width. If the center strip does not measure 1", re-sew both of the seams with a smaller, or larger seam allowance, depending on which you need. When you find the "perfect ¼" seam", layer several pieces of masking tape on the needle plate

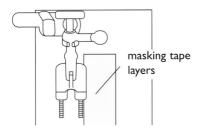

masking tape layers

of your sewing machine to mark the place. Then, when you sew your patches together, your fabric will always meet the masking tape edge, making a consistent seam allowance.

Careful pressing after each step is important as you sew your blocks. Pressing helps to ensure accurate piecing and should be done in an up and down fashion, rather than a side-to-side motion. The objective is to get pieces to lie flat without stretching them. Many quilters make an initial press with their fingers on small unit piecing, then follow up with an iron pressing when a larger unit is pieced. Seams will be pressed to one side as shown on the piecing diagrams. Seams should be pressed toward the darker fabric unless other directions are given.

Now that you're ready to begin, here is more helpful information on the techniques you need to complete your quilt.

Half-Square Triangles

1. Layer two same-sized squares with right sides together. Draw a diagonal pencil line from corner to corner on the lightest square.

2. Sew a scant ¼" on each side of the drawn line.

3. Cut on the drawn line and separate to make two triangle units.

4. Press toward the darker fabric unless instructed otherwise.

Directional Triangles

This method is used when the triangles are always in the same position, such as the dark triangle will always be to the left of the light triangle, or visa versa.

1. Layer two squares with right sides together and draw intersecting diagonal lines from corner to corner as shown.

2. Using a scant ¼" seam, stitch as shown. Rotate block so that you can use the drawn line as a stitching guide. The instructions for each project will tell you whether to stitch on the left or right of the line.

3. Cut along drawn lines and press open.

Quick-Corner Triangles

Quick corner triangles are made by sewing squares to the corners of larger squares or rectangles. The sizes of the squares and rectangles and where to position them is given in each project.

1. On the wrong side of the square that will become the triangle, draw a diagonal line with a pencil and ruler.

2. With right sides together, position this square on the corner of the piece to which you want to add it. Pin and sew on drawn line.

3. Trim the top layer to ¼" from the seam line as shown. Press the remaining triangle toward the corner.

Trim

> **A**nother technique...leaving the original rectangle without trimming helps to keep your pieces square as you add quick corner triangles to them. If your triangle is off slightly, you can use the bottom rectangle as a guide for piecing.

Squaring Up the Blocks

Making sure that your blocks are square as you piece them is important to insure they fit together easily. As you piece them, you may want to square them up as you complete each stage of the square or rectangle. Turn the unit to the wrong side and measure it. Then carefully trim the edges to the correct size.

Before joining the blocks together in rows, be sure to square up or resize your blocks so that they are all the same size. Make all the blocks before you determine your average block size. For example, if the blocks, which should all measure 12½" actually measure 12⅜", you can use the 12⅜" size since they should fit together fine.

If the block looks distorted, repressing may help. If trimming is necessary, trim very carefully and allow the ¼" seam allowance on all sides.

Adding the Borders

Square Corner Borders

Sew the side borders to the quilt first unless the instructions say otherwise.

1. To find the most accurate measurement for the sides, measure the quilt through the center vertically and cut or piece the side border strips to this measurement.

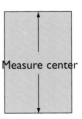

Measure center

2. Fold the quilt in half and then in fourths and mark those points with a pin. Fold and mark the border strips in the same way.

3. With right sides together, pin the strips to the sides matching the marks. Sew the borders to the quilt top and press.

4. To determine the length of the top and bottom borders, measure the quilt horizontally across the center including the borders you just added. Cut or piece the strips to this measurement.

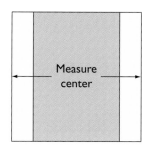

5. As you did for the side borders, fold, mark, and pin the border strips to the quilt. Sew the top and bottom strips to the quilt and press.

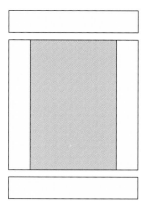

Mitered Borders

1. Just as you did for Square Corner Borders, measure the length of the quilt top vertically through the center. Add two times the width of your border plus 4", and this will be the length to cut the side border strips.

2. Fold the quilt in half and then in fourths and place pins at these points. Fold and mark the border strips in the same way. Mark the measured length of the quilt top on the border strip.

3. With right sides together, pin the strips to the sides of the quilt top matching pins.

4. Starting 1/4" from the edge, sew the borders to the sides of the quilt top, stopping and backstitching 1/4" from the edge.

Stop stitching 1/4" from edge

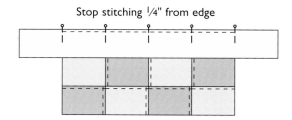

5. For the top and bottom borders, measure the quilt horizontally through the center. Add two times the width of your border plus 4", and this will be the length to cut or piece the top and bottom border strips. The border strips will extend beyond each end and overlap the side borders.

6. To create the miter, work with the quilt right side up and lay one strip on top of the adjacent border.

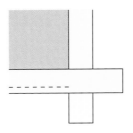

7. Fold the top border under so it meets the edge of the quilt and forms a 45° angle. Press and pin the fold in place.

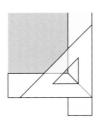

8. Position a 90° triangle or ruler over the corner to check that the corner is flat and square. Press the fold firmly to create a crease.

9. Fold the center section of the top diagonally from the corner, right sides together, and align the long edges of the border strips. On the wrong side, pin the diagonal crease of the borders.

10. Beginning at the inside corner, backstitch and stitch along the crease toward the outside point, being careful not to stretch the fabric. Backstitch at the end. Trim the excess border fabric to ¼". Press the seam to one side. Repeat to complete all four corners.

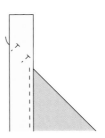

Finishing the Quilt

Layering and Basting

Before layering your quilt top, batting, and backing, press the entire top. Be sure to snip any long or raveling threads from the back to prevent them from showing through the quilt top. With the wrong side of the backing up, layer the batting on top of the backing. Place the quilt top, right side up on the batting. Smooth all layers out, creating a flat, even, wrinkle-free surface.

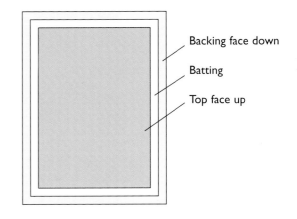

Backing face down

Batting

Top face up

If you choose to hand quilt, baste the layers together with cotton basting thread in horizontal and vertical rows approximately 6"–8" apart. If you choose to machine quilt, safety pins can be used to baste the layers. Space them 4"–6" apart.

Machine Quilting

For best results, use a walking foot and a needle designed for machine quilting. Loosen the top tension of your machine by one-half of a number setting to prevent the bottom thread from being pulled up to the top. The top thread can be cotton, cotton wrapped polyester, or monofilament nylon. I match thread color and weight of the top and bobbin to achieve uniform stitches and to prevent the bottom color from showing on the quilt top. To avoid tying threads and to secure quilting lines, begin and end with several very small stitches.

Hand Quilting

For hand quilting I recommend a between needle, size 9–12, and cotton quilting thread. Secure the quilt in a freestanding frame or a lap hoop and draw it taut. Thread the needle and make a small knot on the end, trimming the tail to about 1/8". Push the needle through the quilt top and batting 3/4" to 1" away from the place you intend to start quilting. Gently pull the knot under the fabric, securing it in the batting. If the knot continues to come back up through the top, make a bigger knot or try to start your quilting at a seam, securing the knot in the seam allowance. Push the needle straight down with a thimble. Come up a short distance away and make a rock-

ing motion with the needle to create several short running stitches.

Adding a Sleeve

If you plan to hang your quilt, sew a hanging sleeve to the top at the time the binding is added. Cut a 7"-wide strip of fabric that is an inch shorter in length than the width of the quilt top. Turn under the ends of the strip 1/2" and machine stitch. Then, with wrong sides together, fold the strip lengthwise and press.

Center the sleeve at the top edge of the quilt back, matching the unfinished edges and pin. Using a scant 1/4" seam allowance, sew in place. You may want to pin the folded edge to the quilt back to keep it from getting caught in the seam when sewing on the binding. After completing the binding, hand sew the bottom of the sleeve to the back.

Quilt back

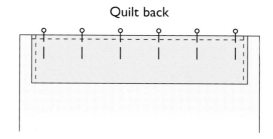

Binding

Sew the binding strips together, end-to-end with a diagonal seam, to make one continuous strip. Press under one end of the strip ¼". Fold the pieced strip lengthwise, wrong sides together and press.

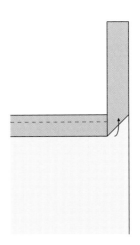

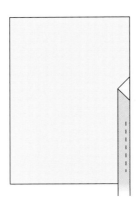

Matching raw edges, place the beginning of the binding about half way down one side edge on the front of the quilt. Begin stitching about 3" away from the end of the binding, using a few backstitches and a scant ¼" seam. Leave the beginning 3" unstitched for now.

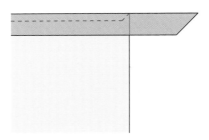

Stop ¼" away from the first corner, backstitch, and with the needle still in the quilt, pivot 45°. Then, sew to the corner of the quilt and backstitch.

Lift the needle and fold the binding strip up at right angles. Fold it back down even with the edge of the quilt. Begin sewing at the folded edge and repeat this step at each corner.

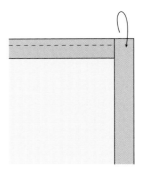

When sewing along the top edge of the quilt, sew the sleeve to the back of the quilt at the same time the binding is sewn to the front.

Stop sewing 3" from the beginning point, backstitch, and remove the quilt from the sewing machine. Trim the binding end at an angle leaving enough fabric to tuck into the beginning, folded end.

Finish sewing the binding to the quilt. Turn the folded edge to the back side of the quilt and hand stitch in place. If you have added a sleeve to your quilt, hand sew the folded bottom to the quilt back.

About the Author

❖ ❖

Never content to leave a quilt in its simplest form, Claudia Olson has always looked for ways to make it more interesting. Not long after she began quilting about 14 years ago, she discovered she wasn't happy just following someone else's instructions. She began the process of creating new quilt patterns and quilt settings of her own.

Her fascination with two-block quilts was sparked when she was a student of popular quilter, Marsha McCloskey. After developing some of her own methods and ideas, she began sharing them through teaching quilt classes and presentations to her local quilt group.

In the year 2000 she enlisted the help of her quilt group friends to sew the quilts she had designed, and the end result was her first book, *15 Two-Block Quilts*. A native of California and a graduate of California State University at Fullerton, Claudia now resides in Wenatchee, Washington, with her family.

Index

❖ ❖

OTHER FINE BOOKS FROM C&T PUBLISHING

For more information write for a free catalog:
C&T Publishing, Inc.
P.O. Box 1456
Lafayette, CA 94549
(800) 284-1114
E-mail: ctinfo@ctpub.com
Website: www.ctpub.com

For quilting supplies:
Cotton Patch Mail Order
3405 Hall Lane, Dept.CTB
Lafayette, CA 94549
(800) 835-4418
(925) 283-7883
E-mail:quiltusa@yahoo.com
Website: www.quiltusa.com

Note: Fabrics used in the quilts shown may not be currently available since fabric manufacturers keep most fabrics in print for only a short time.